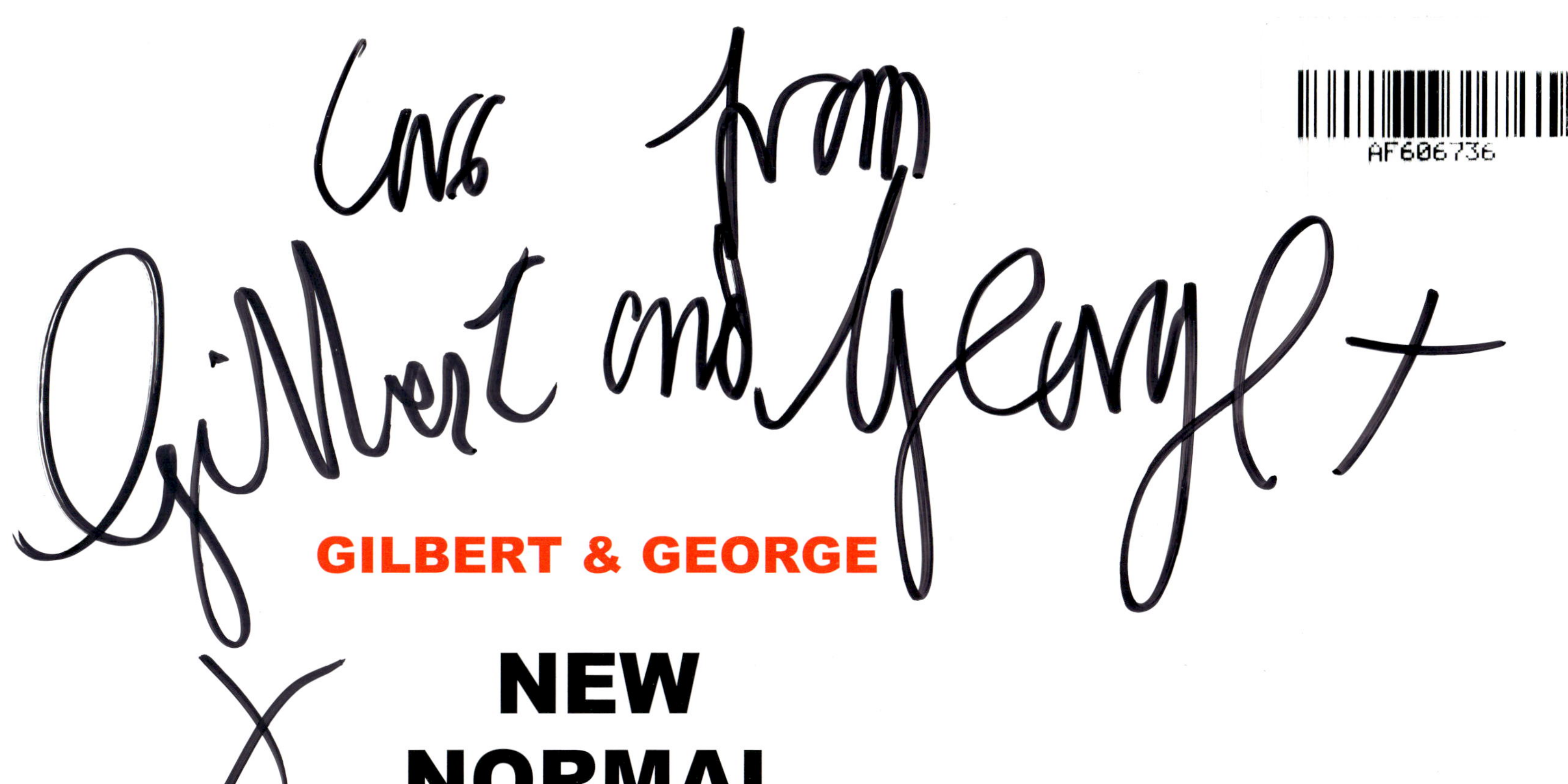

GILBERT & GEORGE

NEW NORMAL PICTURES

PARIS

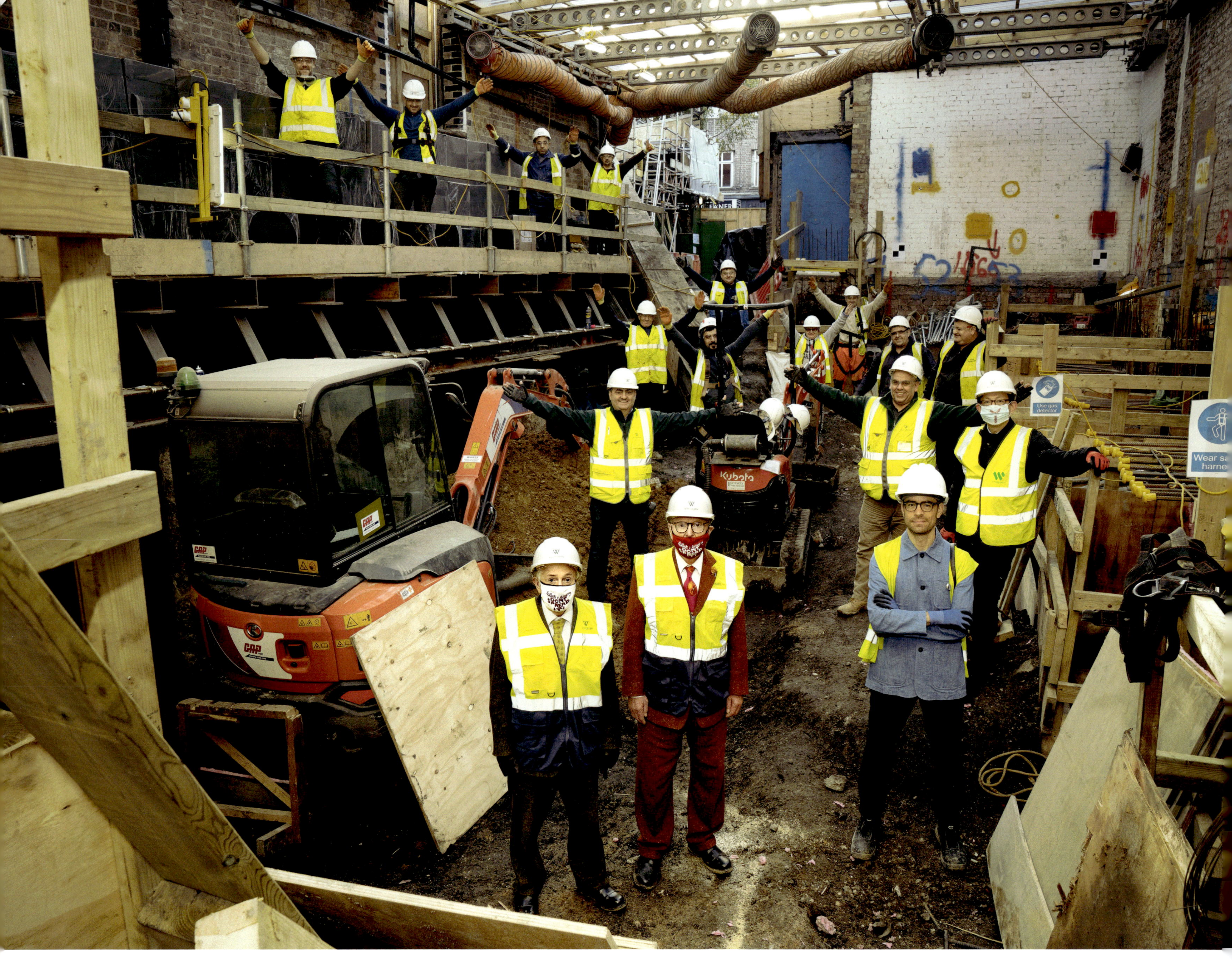

WORK IN PROGRESS, 2020. The Artists, Manuel Irsara the Architect, Yu Yigang, and the team here at the future Gilbert & George Centre. Photo: Tom Oldham

GILBERT & GEORGE

NEW NORMAL PICTURES

PARIS

30 MAY to 31 JULY 2021

THADDAEUS ROPAC
69 Avenue du Général Leclerc

ropac.net

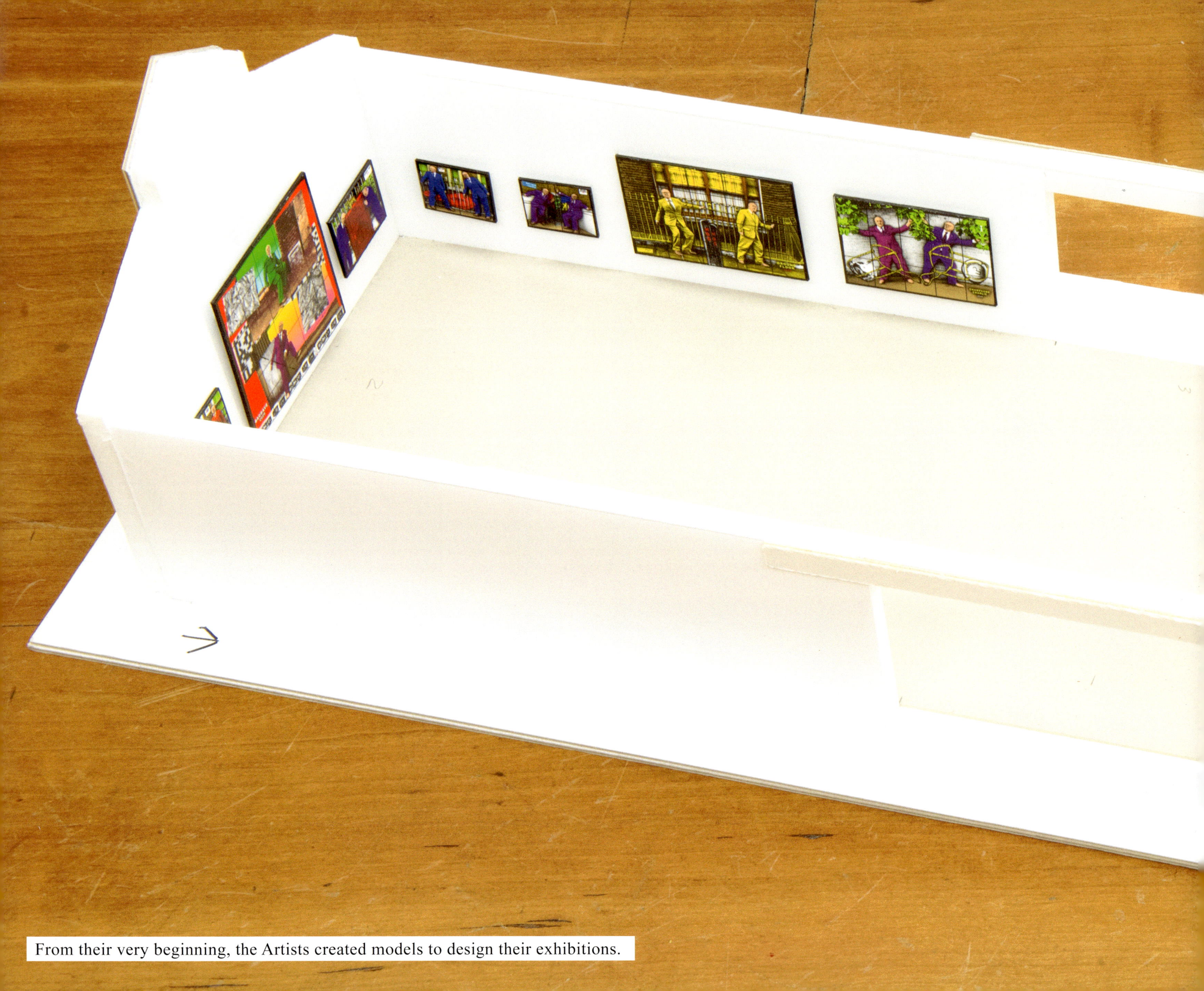

From their very beginning, the Artists created models to design their exhibitions.

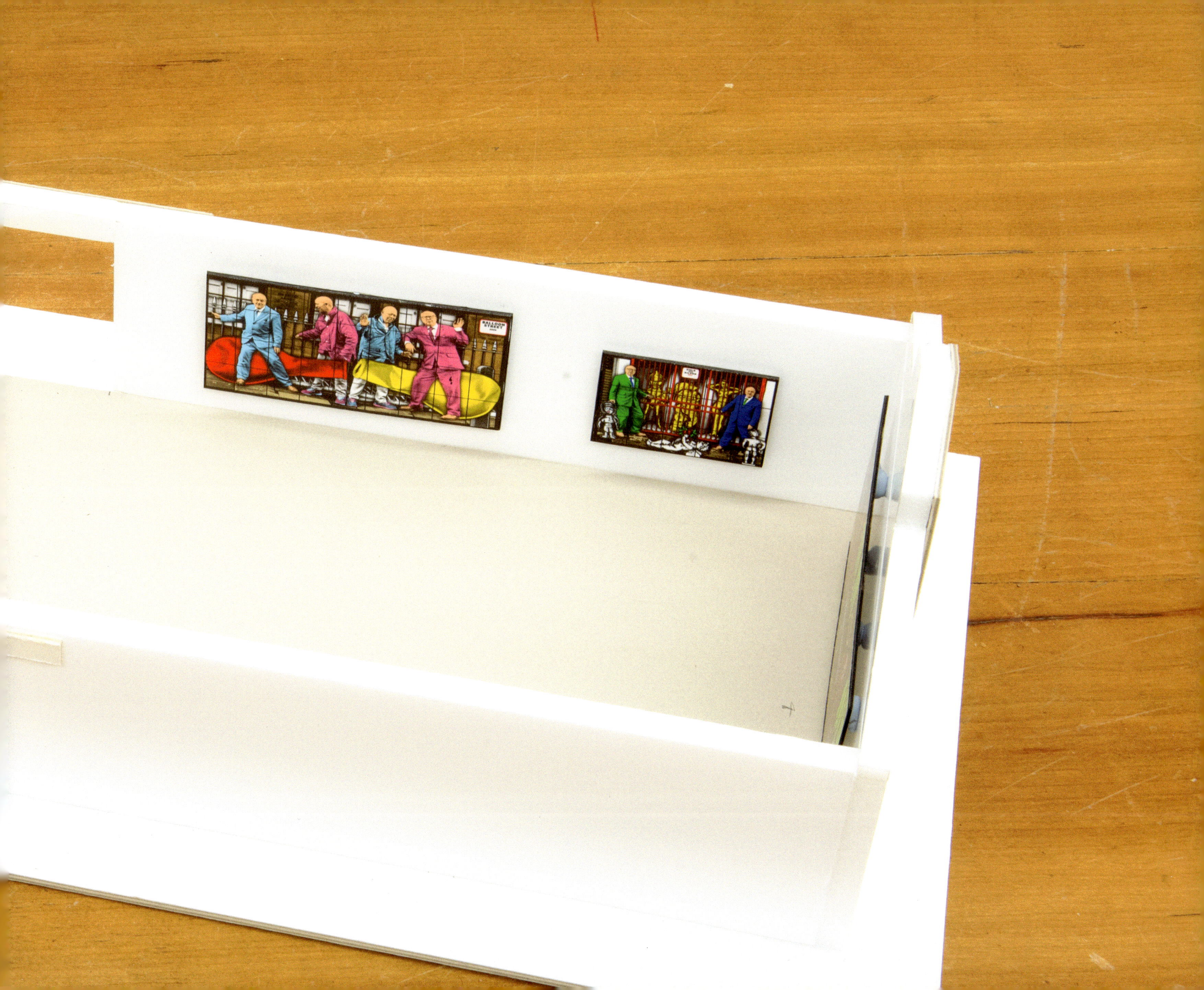
BALLOON
STREET

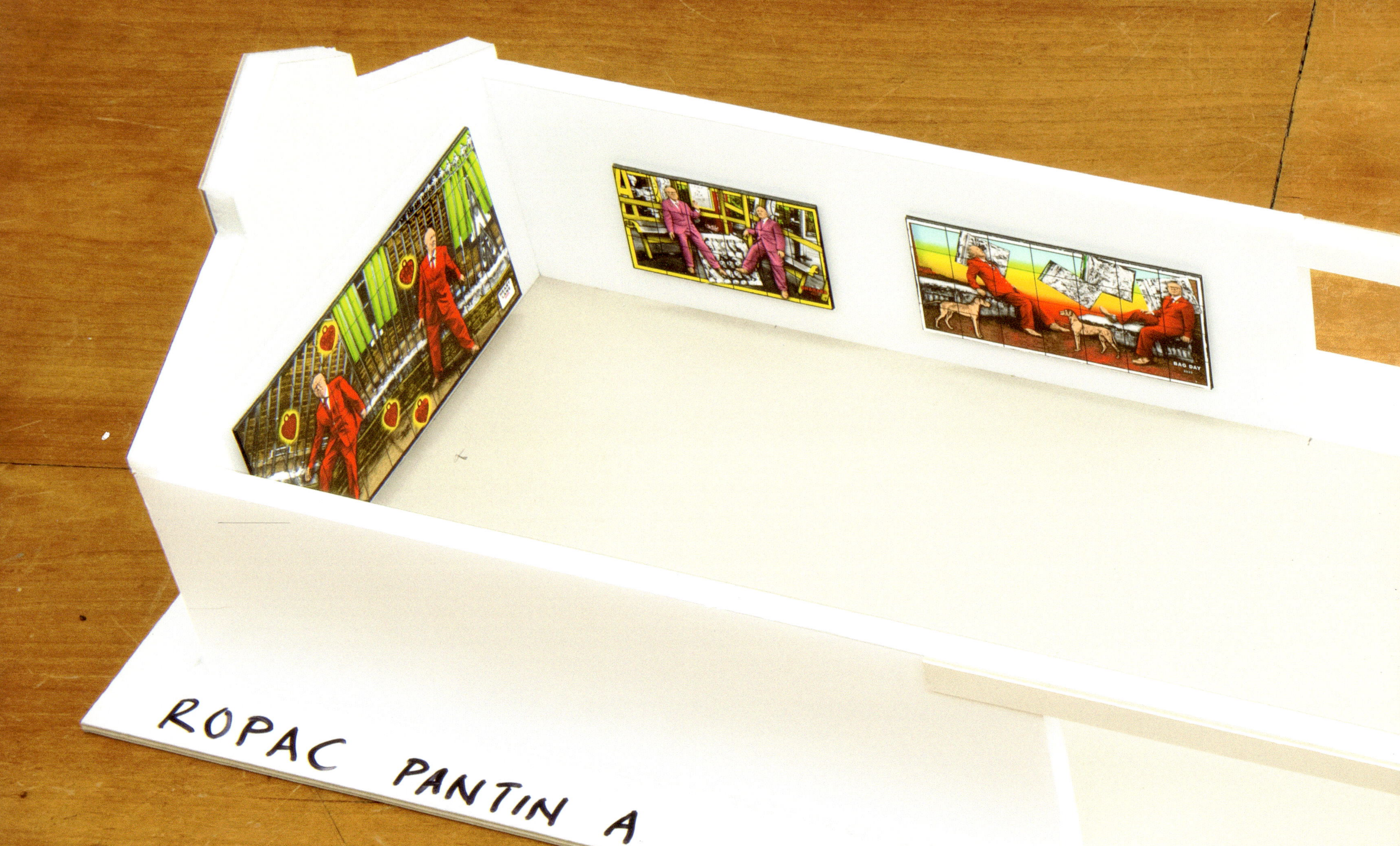
ROPAC PANTIN A

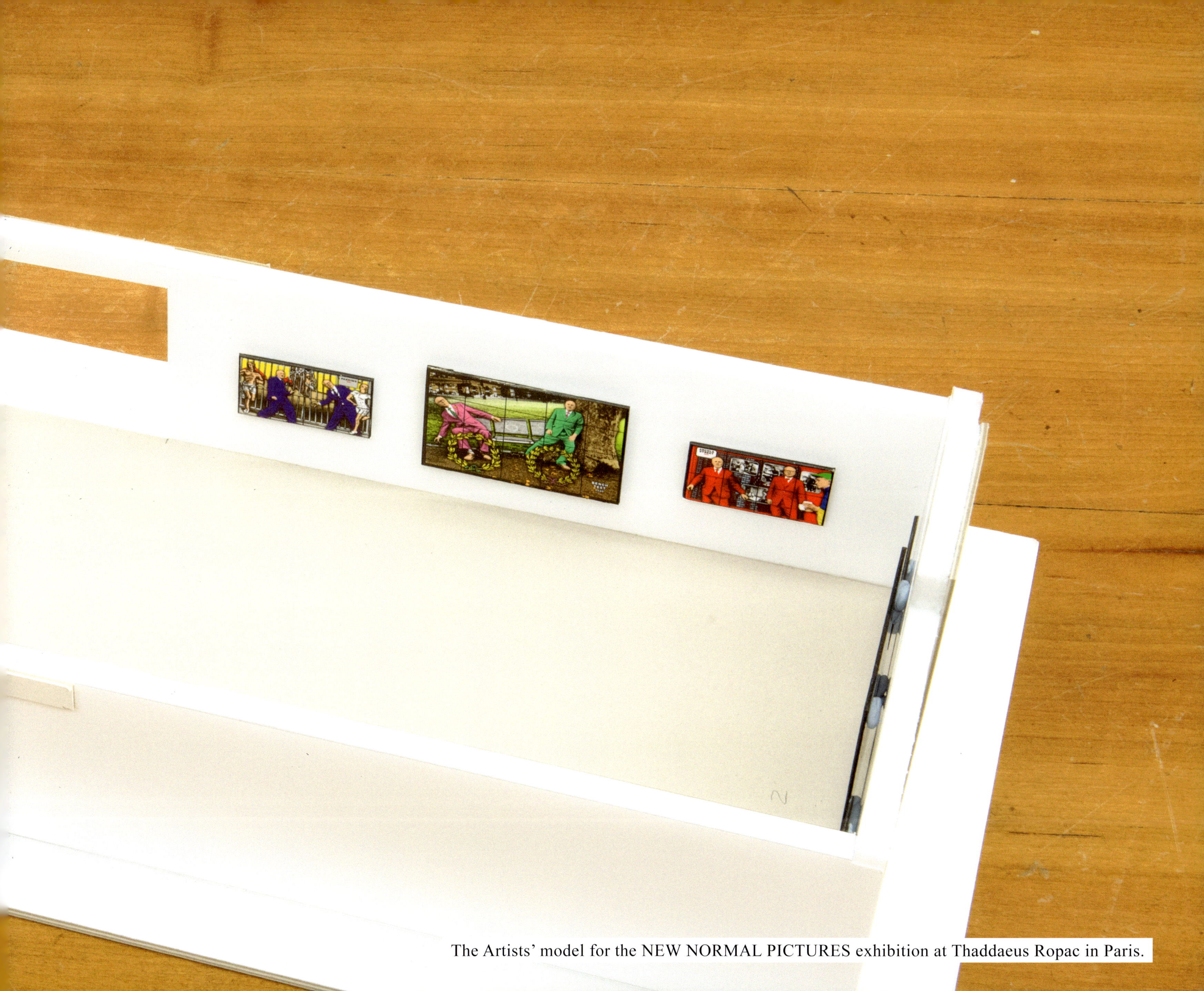

The Artists' model for the NEW NORMAL PICTURES exhibition at Thaddaeus Ropac in Paris.

NEW NORMAL PICTURES
IN THE EXHIBITION

BAGRAVE
CHAMPAGNE CHARLIE
BENCH TEST
DIG
GOLD AND SILVER
BAG DAY
TOYNBEE ROAD
PARKING
ARCOLA STREET

BALLOON STREET
230V AC
GROUND FLOOR
JUST STREET
NO 10
GARDEN WAY
NORMAL SERVICE
MOSS CLOSE
SHANARA

HEART LANE

GILBERT & GEORGE
NEW NORMAL PICTURES
2020

Michael Bracewell

"Let us go then, you and I,
When the evening is spread out against the sky
Like a patient etherized upon a table;
Let us go, through certain half-deserted streets..."

'The Love Song of J. Alfred Prufrock.'
T. S. Eliot, 1920.

Since meeting as students in the late summer of 1967, Gilbert & George have been travelling together on a visionary and moral journey that they liken to 'The Pilgrim's Progress'.

This journey is made on foot along the endless streets of London; occasionally by bus to the city's eastern edges. New-build developments on reclaimed and reworked land; excursions into a not-too-distant future, as mild as it is lowering.

These "NEW NORMAL PICTURES' pictures have the air, also, of temperate yet strangely intense days. In fact, the stages on a journey they seem to recount have a "post-everything" air; as though Gilbert & George have just crossed through a fissure in time to a place that is almost but not quite familiar – a place that looks normal but is not normal, is skewed, perhaps abandoned.

Here are the artists on 'BAG DAY'. The artists appear stranded on stone benches or tombstones, a psychedelic sunset or sunrise behind them. A sense of other-worldly awakening. Each is attended by what seems like a ceremonial hound. Gilbert & George could be resting on their long journey. Behind them are four small, sealable plastic bags – drug bags.

What is it about these drug bags that gives them the air of being the lowest form of litter? They look dirty, abject – discard of the meanest and most joyless kind. With amazed (George) and wary (Gilbert) expressions, the artists look as though they have just materialised for this BAG DAY from another dimension.

We see them thus in 'BAGRAVE' – those same expressions of the newly and suddenly arrived. Attempting to get bearings or defensive or alert. The existentially displaced – individuals thrown into a reality not of their choosing, frighteningly free to make sense of it as best they can. Railings and drug bags and bin bags and waste cardboard. A few autumn leaves from the tree overhanging the artists.

Gilbert & George bring worlds to life in their art that are also moods and feelings. Brute realism is infused with the vague yet precise temper of disquieting and uneasy dreams. The artists often use very few elements – a concentrate of concise image-subjects – to create the violence, drama and mystery in their pictures. Here, litter, railings, drug bags, shovels and old trinkets become like a 'palette' – primal images that do the work of primary colours. There are no ambiguous shades; no finesse or subtlety softens their bleak urban other-worldliness.

In these 'NEW NORMAL PICTURES' it feels as though the old punk adage, 'the day the world turned Day-Glo', has come to life. Everywhere is dark yet too bright, borderline deranged.

Tonal contrasts go to war with one another; as in 'MOSS CLOSE' or 'SHANARA', for instance, in which the artists in their purple and mauve suits appear in the former picture to be cornered against beaten up utility casing, tagged in primary colours. In the latter encountered on a bus stop bench – confusion of struts in car paint yellow. The graffiti 'CRACK 4 SEX' is tagged SHANARA. Between the artists a drug bag printed with uniform skulls.

The 'NEW NORMAL PICTURES' depict streets and alleys and vistas where the unreal city seems to rearrange time and tenses: accelerating the slow; stalling the immediate. The overlooked and thrown away, too, reacquire visibility and meaning. The usual hierarchies reverse: discard dominates.

The journey on foot – "through certain half-deserted streets" – is also the vision of Gilbert & George, that is their art, of which they are the embodiment. A vision that is lived, walked and recounted as feelings and atmospheres, like dreams walking in broad daylight or a ceaselessly unwinding scroll or frieze of immense length, narrative and mysterious, confrontational and arcane.

Writing for a journal based in Baltimore, back in the late 1990s, I likened Gilbert & George to "Modernist extensions of Dickensian characters". In the intervening years I have felt no need to adjust this description. The artists see – as did Charles Dickens – the creases and shadows and fractures in ordinary life where the mood of the city takes on its own sentience. And thus they also share with the Modernist sensibility that keen, overwhelming awareness of the psychic and the psychological, the moral allegory.

With visceral intensity the 'NEW NORMAL PICTURES' convey a disturbed mood that seems to be one of apprehension and expectancy, that is confounded by an unknown and unanswerable question. This 'condition' seems to stalk, menace and haunt Gilbert & George in this drugged up, litter strewn world in which grave-digger shovels, trinkets and semi precious stones – see for example, 'GOLD AND SILVER' or 'DIG' – appear like tokens in a computer game.

The art of Gilbert & George is an art of feelings, emotions and intellect. The streets around the artists' ceremonial home in Spitalfields in London's East End can still bare their teeth with Victorian menace; even as the gutters and alleys are strewn with the debris of drugs so twenty-first century that they seem to have fallen from the pages of science fiction.

In the 'NEW NORMAL PICTURES' it feels as though the Modernist and the Dickensian and the science-fictional combine in the life-as-art-as-endless journeying that is the vision of Gilbert & George.

Shame, depression, love, loneliness, intoxication, fear, dreams, aloneness, stillness and vertigo. The viewer experiences the brutality and strangeness of the art of Gilbert & George as also a mad-mystical-visionary commentary upon the mood of the modern world: its momentum and restlessness, nervousness and grind. The locked doors and rain slippery pavements, the mad calligraphy of cryptic anonymous statements scrawled angrily in doorways; the collapse of meaning into primal or cosmic forces.

In these 'NEW NORMAL PICTURES', railing and walls and bins and litter are everywhere; the damp and the dirt are sometimes bejewelled with clusters of ornate trinkets and baubles; brightly suited Gilbert & George are watchful, tense, exhausted, resting, dead-headed – as if they've been awake for years. Colour and monochrome contrast, making metal look harder, brick coarser and plastic colder and more chemical. Drugs and oblivion hang in the air like damp.

It has been argued, successfully and frequently – even in the revision notes for the English Literature GCSE – that modern poetry begins with T. S. Eliot's famous image (from 'The Love Song of J Alfred Prufrock', quoted at the beginning of this essay) likening the evening sky to "a patient etherized upon a table."

In these few words science not only pervades the sublime but puts it to sleep. The Romantic and the surgical combine; the elegiac and anesthetised and gently indifferent universe.

The literary Modernists – of whom Eliot is usually reckoned foremost – specialised in prophecy and premonition rather like grave doctors with a sideline in research. Occasionally forecasts would be declaimed, quietly, bureaucratically, but with utmost certainty. The modern urban world, they saw, was criss-crossed by soft shadows and sudden breezes that doubled as mystical, allegorical, occult and spiritual occurrences.

In this new normality it is as though two cities – let us say two Londons – exist side by side, nearly but not quite in step and for the most part invisible to one another. But occasionally the membrane between them thins and parts for long enough to reveal the visionary city, that is where the individual, existentially, sees their moral place – their truth, you could say – within the continuum of time that is also the city; and that oddly and out of nowhere in the middle of the busy ordinary day, becomes universal.

The art of Gilbert & George is the ceaseless traverse between these two cities; and they have been walking for decades, rather as though they were walking these streets before we arrived and will be walking them long after we've left.

Eliot envisaged such walks (he worked not far away, in Moorgate) in the celebrated invitation that opens 'Prufrock' – "Let us go then, you and I…" And shared, it feels, the urban and cosmic geography traversed by Gilbert & George: "Streets that follow like a tedious argument… …To lead you to an overwhelming question." This "overwhelming question" appears to be existential; as four stanzas on Eliot's avatar asks, "Do I dare disturb the universe?"

The line could describe the mix of apprehension and agitation that pervades the 'NEW NORMAL PICTURES'. Against railings and litter and shrubberies and household detritus, flanked by ominous spades or shovels and framed by the dumped little plastic drug bags printed with folksy cannabis leaves, smiley faces, pistols and silhouettes of pin-up girls, Gilbert & George still stare fearfully and watchfully, baffled, tense and defiant.

Attended by spirit like old trinkets or backed by those bright gigantic balloons used to inhale nitrous oxide ('№ 10' or 'HEART LANE') the artists freeze, totter, lean and crouch; or slump into empty-headed vacancy, indeed as though etherised upon a table – against chemical orange sky above the city.

In 'ARCOLA STREET' the artists gaze towards the viewer, seeing or unseeing, whilst behind them on pulled down railing shutters are four black and white snap shots of staffs in a cheerful restaurant. In one we see Gilbert & George with two friendly waiters. It is like we are seeing the artists in a former life – before they entered the paranoid baffled world that is the new normality of the 'NEW NORMAL PICTURES'.

This new normality also has an air of Purgatory; a worn-out thoroughfare on the Pilgrim's Progress of Gilbert & George – a place such as you might once have found beneath the walls of ancient cities, home to the discarded and the derelict.

The nineteenth century Danish philosopher, Soren Kierkegaard (popularly known as 'the grandfather of Existentialism') asks,

"If there were no eternal consciousness in a man, if at the bottom of everything there were only a wild ferment, a power that twisting in dark passions produced everything great or inconsequential; if an unfathomable, insatiable emptiness lay hid beneath everything, what would life be but despair?"

And existentialists have a word, 'Facticity', for this condition. It means that: "We find ourselves existing in a world not of our own making and indifferent to our concerns. We are not the source of our existence, but find ourselves thrown into a world we don't control and didn't choose."

The art of Gilbert & George is existential in its assertion of brute realism: the autonomous individual defined by their decisions.

The art of Gilbert & George conveys expressions and representations of individual decisions and belief systems of all kinds. As they take their place in their art, Gilbert & George appear impassive, spectral, respectable, fearful and possessed. They are witness-participants within the visionary world of their art; they become agents of the scenes they traverse. They channel atmospheres rather than make pronouncements. In this they resemble the indwelling 'spirits' of each of their pictures.

If there is a unifying 'temper' to the art of Gilbert & George it derives from this moral vision, in which the modern condition is seen as chaotic and poetic – a matter of indifference to the universe or fate; without meaning save that which the individual creates for himself and for which he alone is responsible.

Meaning, on the journey of life-as-art of Gilbert & George, derives from the psychic traces left by time that are reanimated by the light, chance or the weather. Life goes on. An array of feelings and atmospheres, from liberated soaring wonder to isolation, 'facticity' and angst.

In 1956, Walter Kaufman wrote: "The refusal to belong to any school of thought, the repudiation of the adequacy of any body of beliefs whatever, and especially of systems, and a marked dissatisfaction with traditional philosophy as superficial, academic and remote from life – that is the heart of existentialism."

And the art of Gilbert & George is existential, conveying the intensity of constantly renewed normality. Their art is an active engagement with the nature of freedom and choice; with the volatility, alienation and randomness of modern life as it is bounded by technology, borderlines, and beliefs.

NEW NORMAL PICTURES

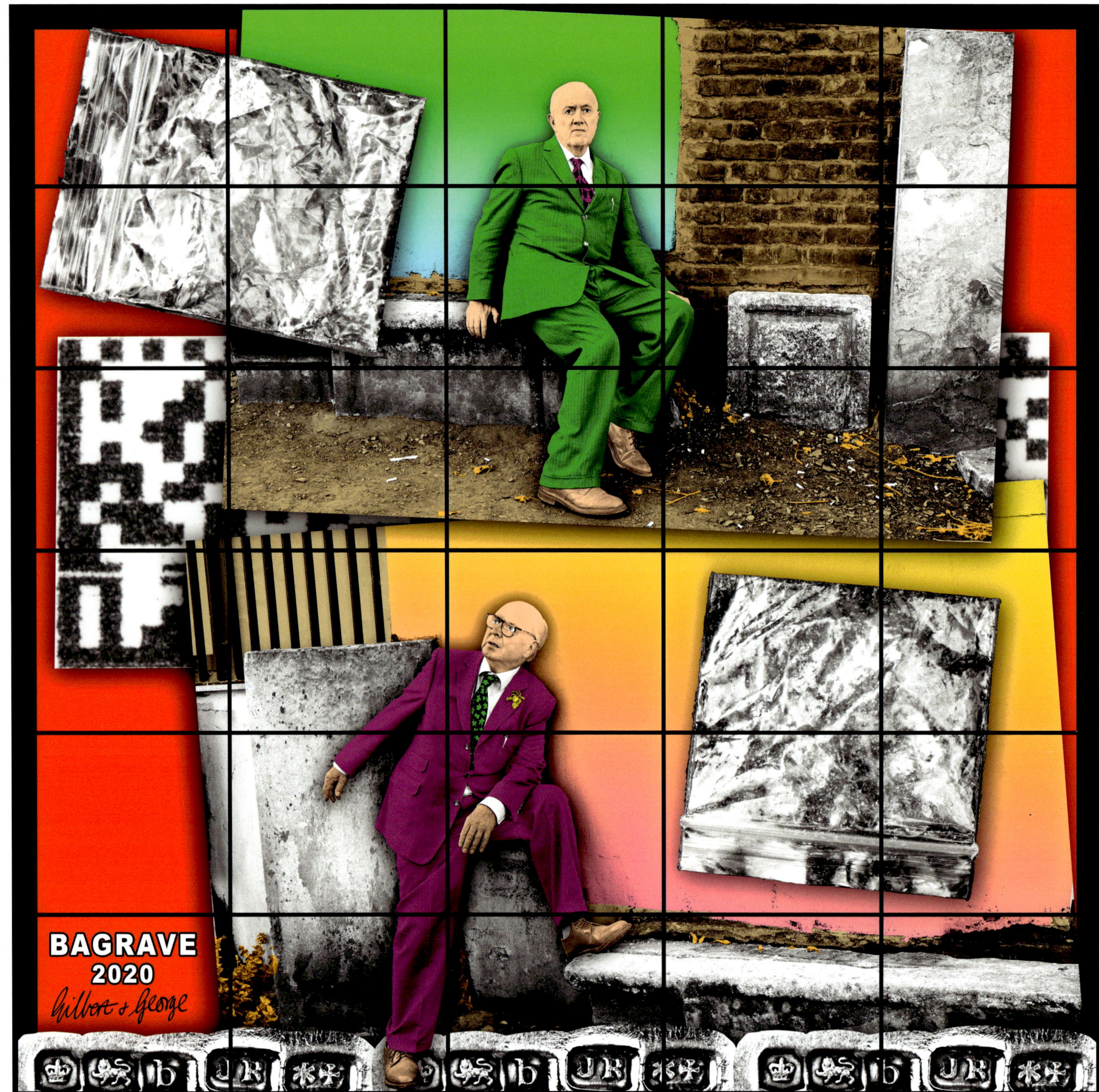

BAGRAVE.
2020.
381 x 377 cm

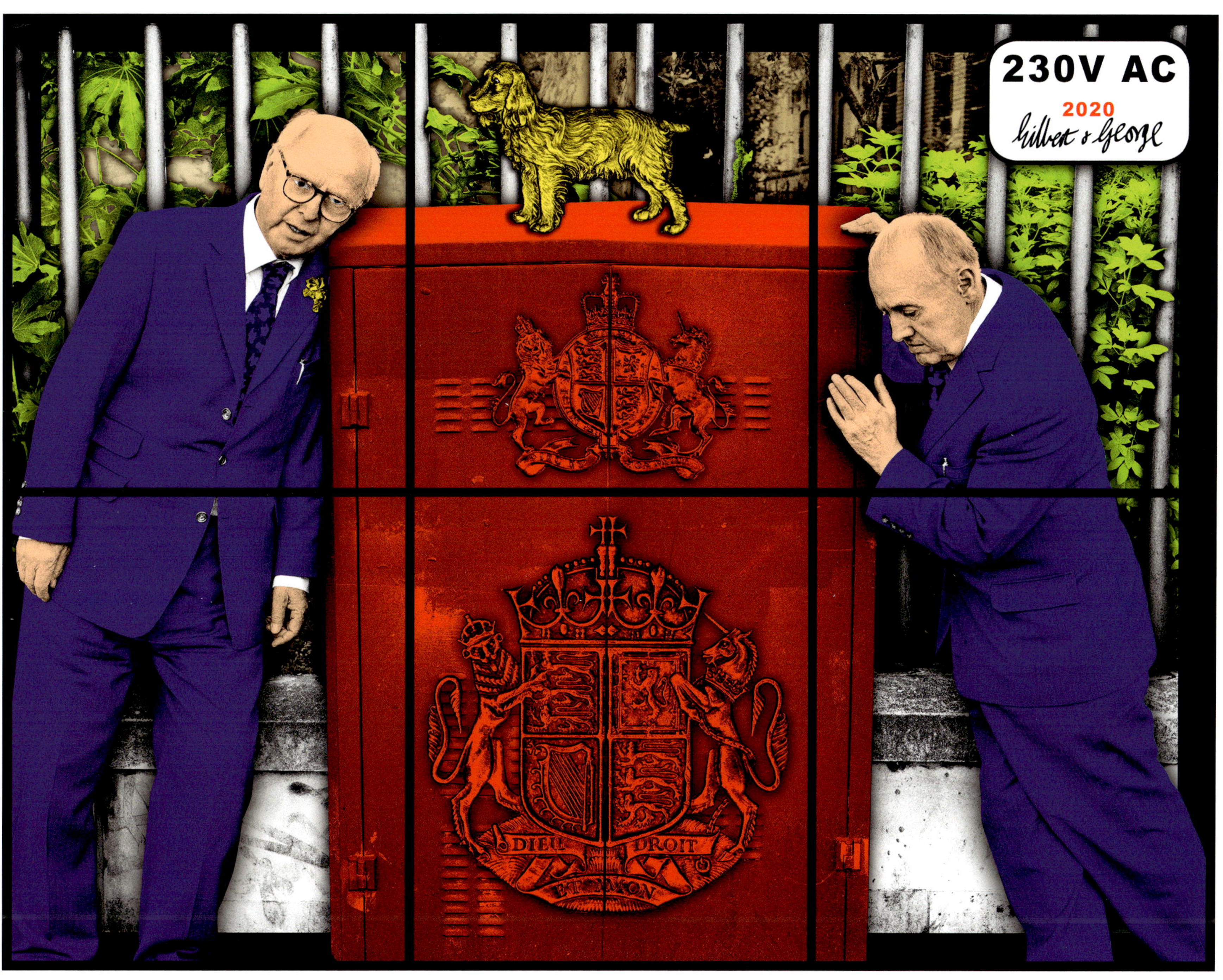

230V AC. 2020. 151 x 191 cm

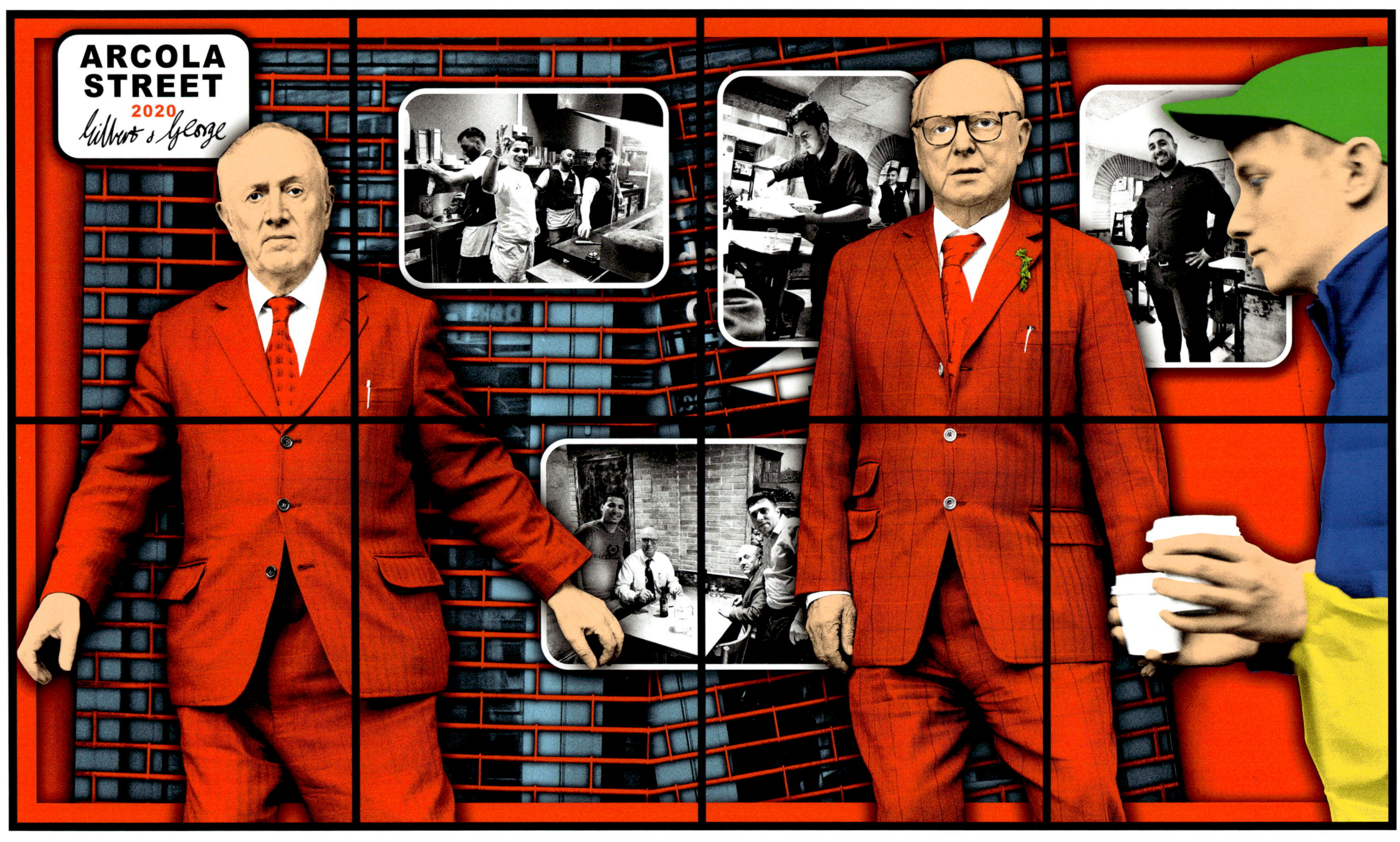

ARCOLA STREET. 2020. 151 x 254 cm

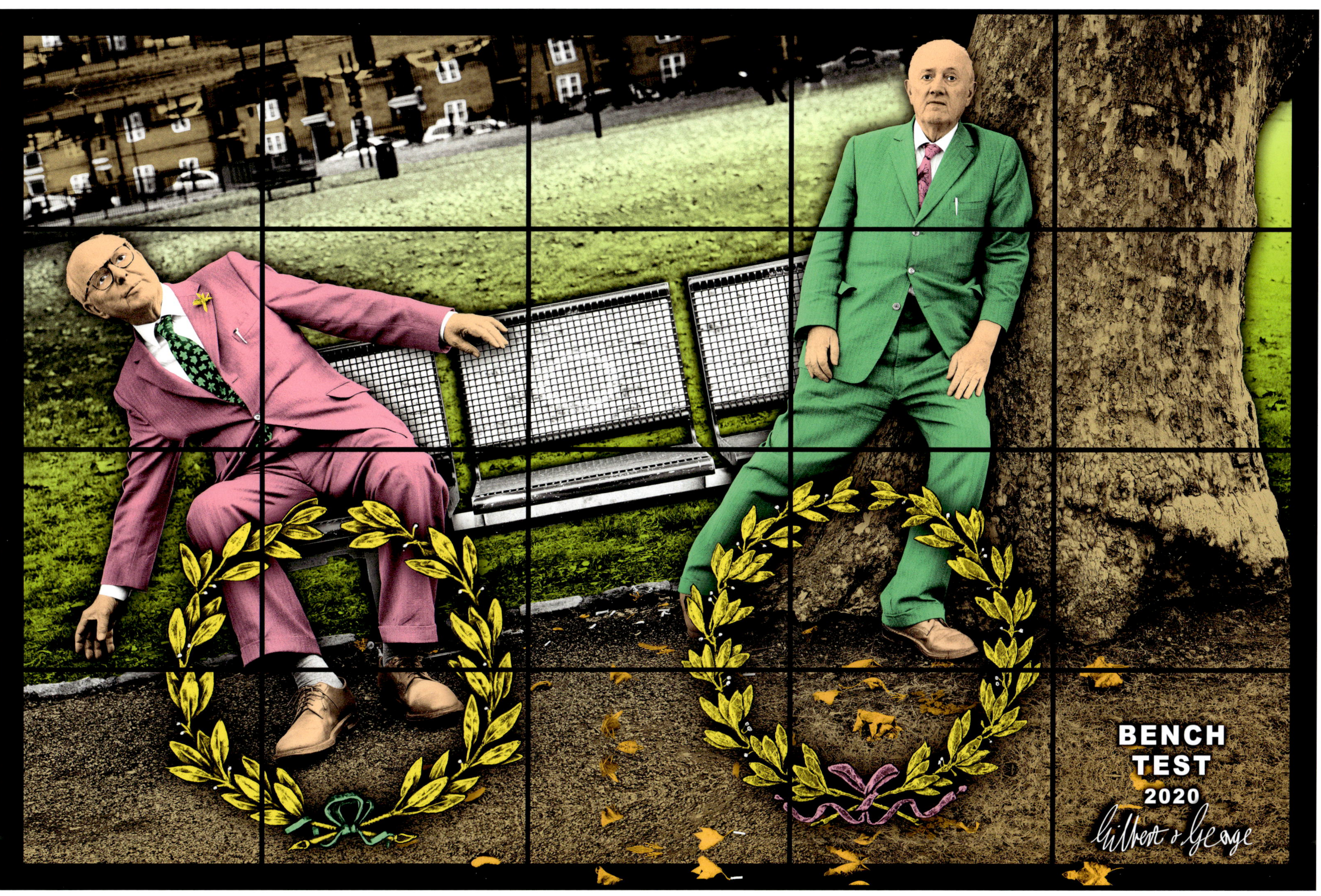

BENCH TEST. 2020. 254 x 378 cm

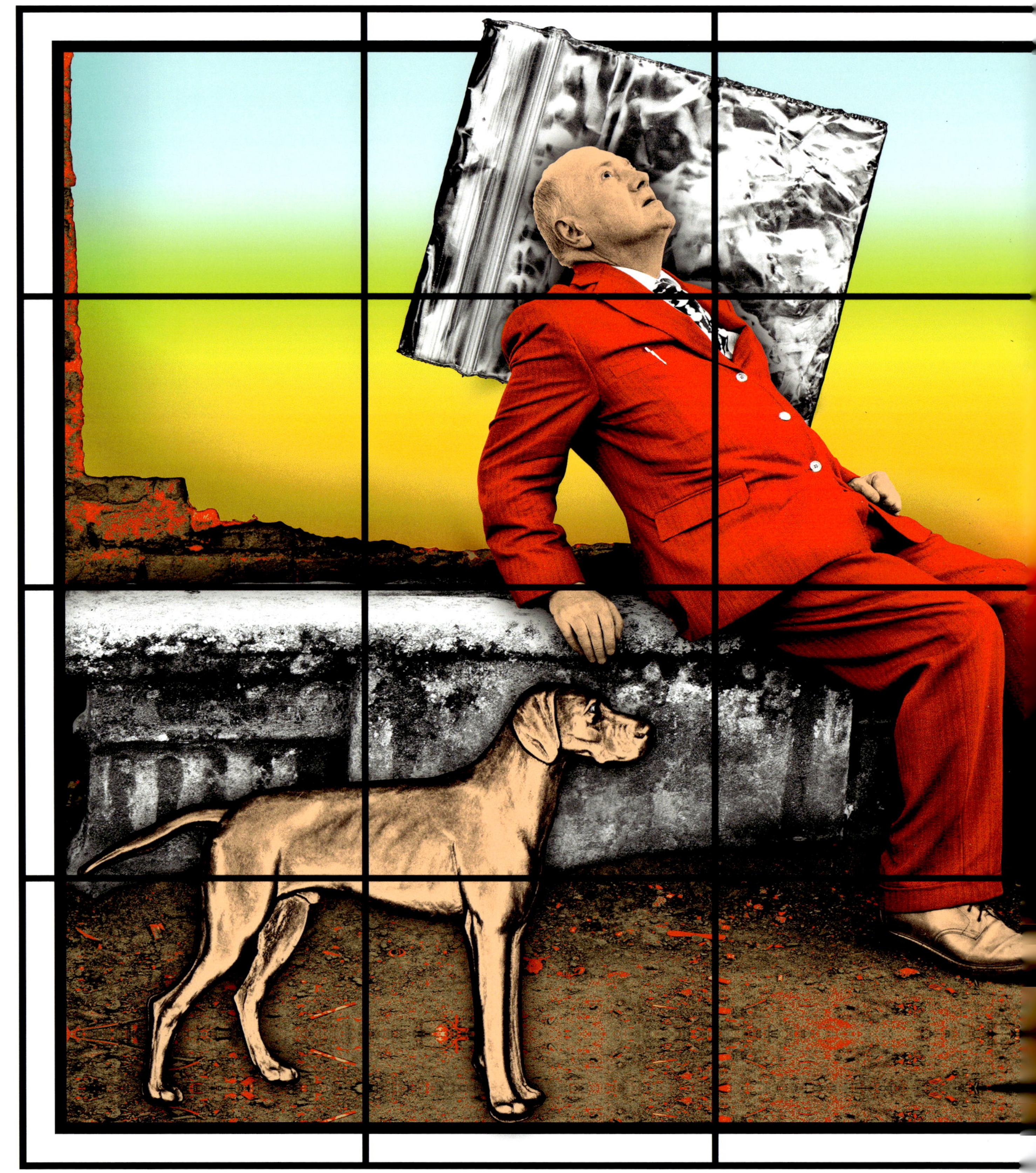

BAG DAY. 2020. 254 x 528 cm

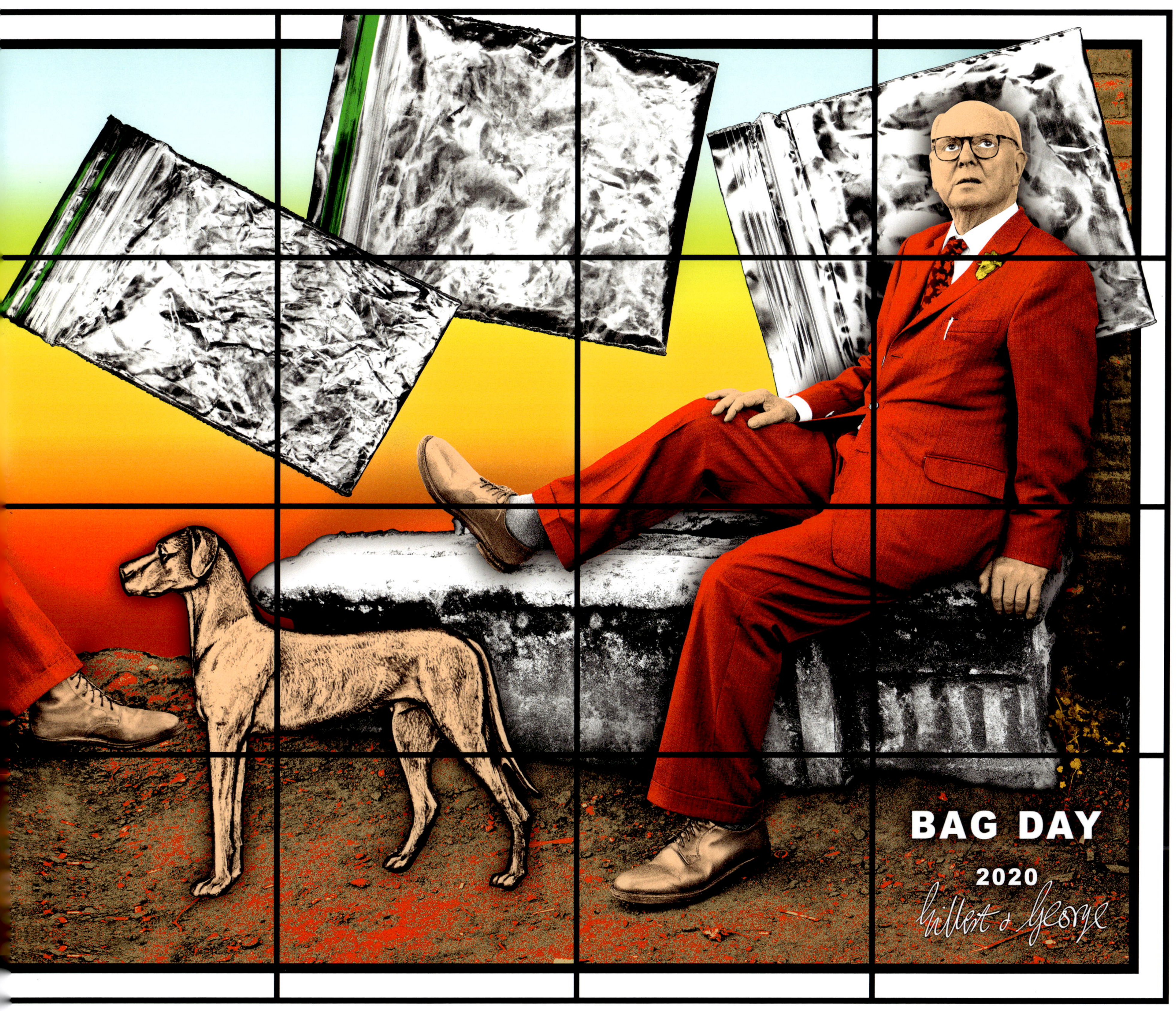
BAG DAY
2020
Gilbert & George

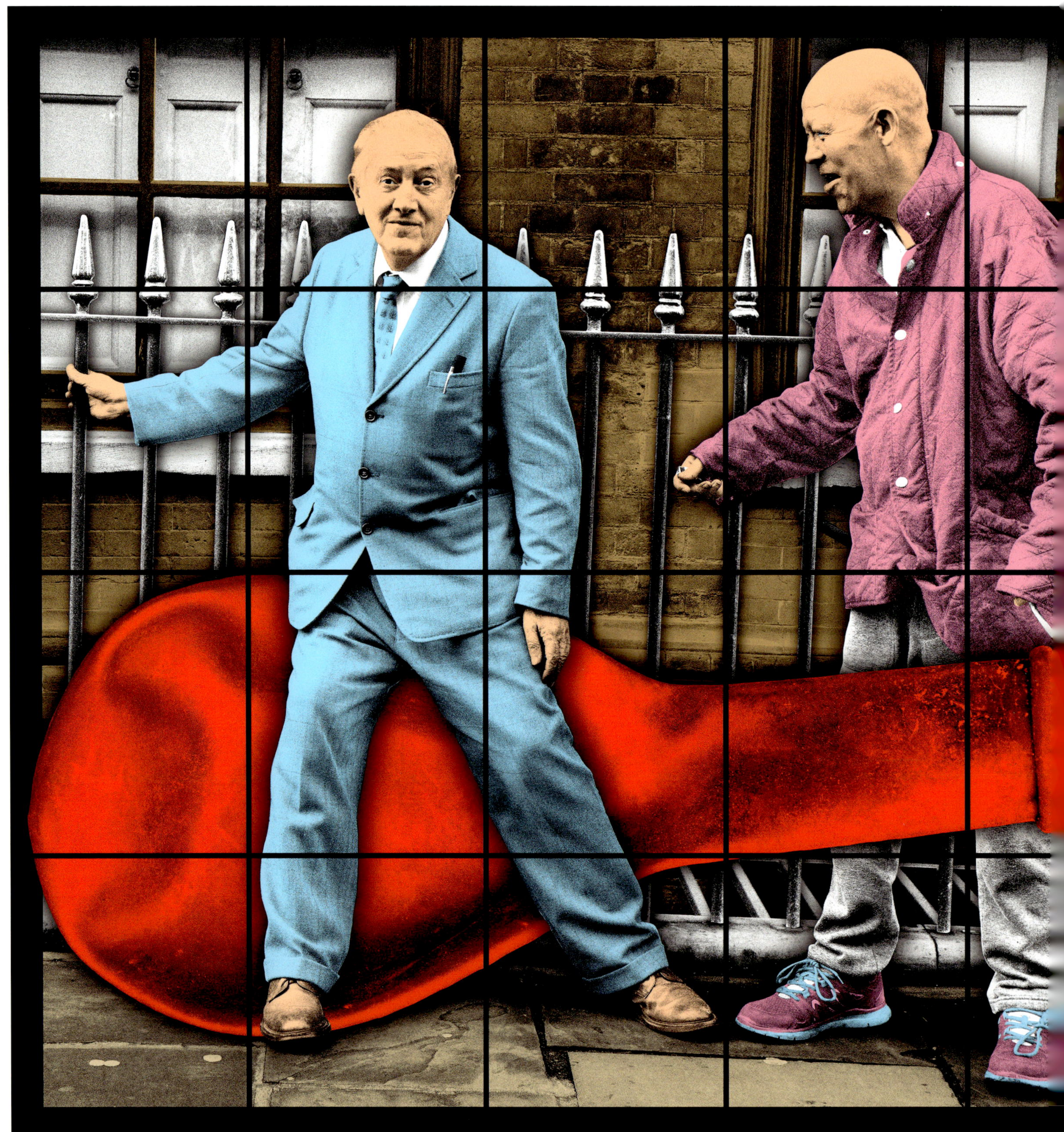

BALLOON STREET.
2020.
302 x 571 cm

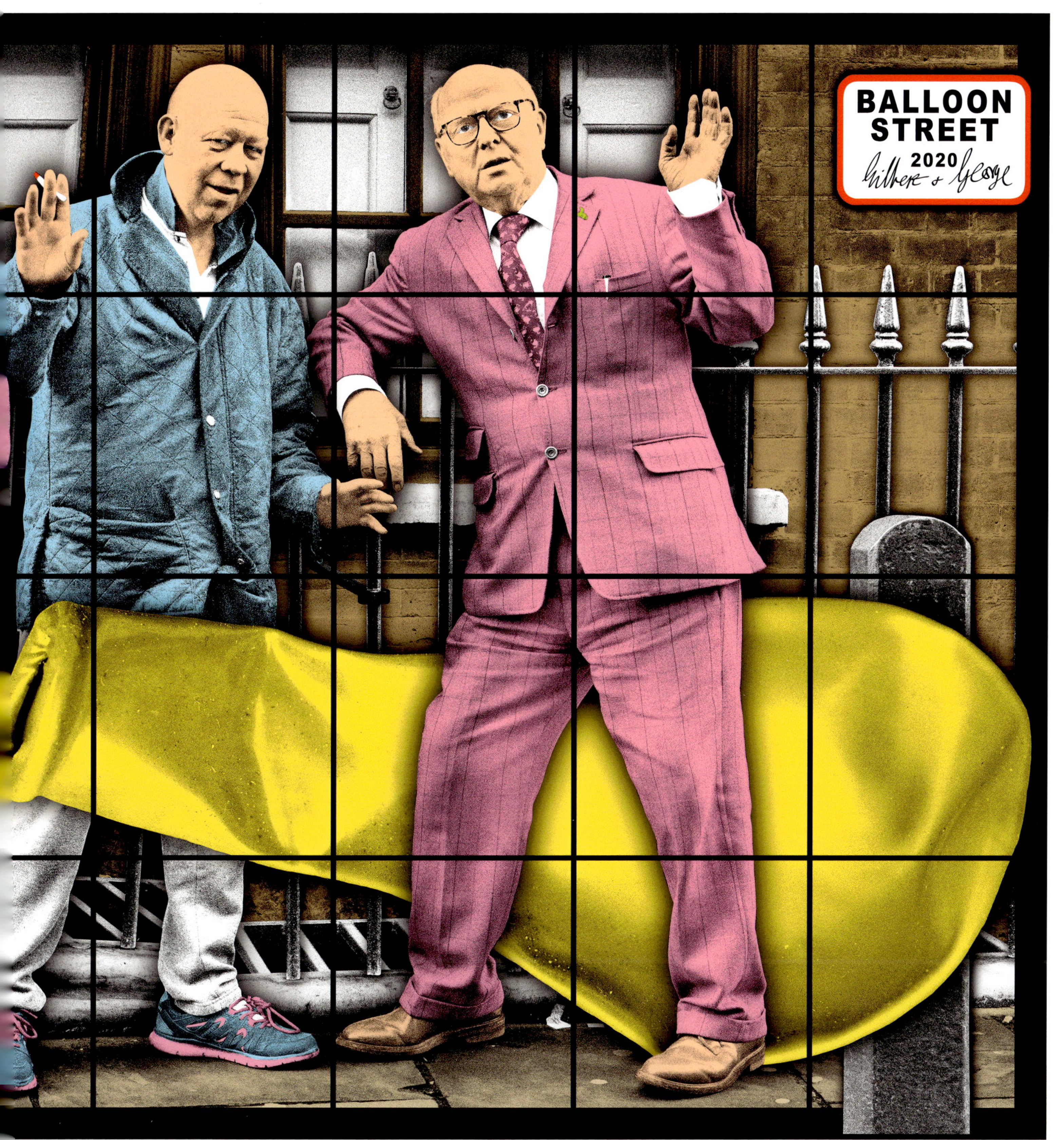
BALLOON
STREET
2020
Gilbert & George

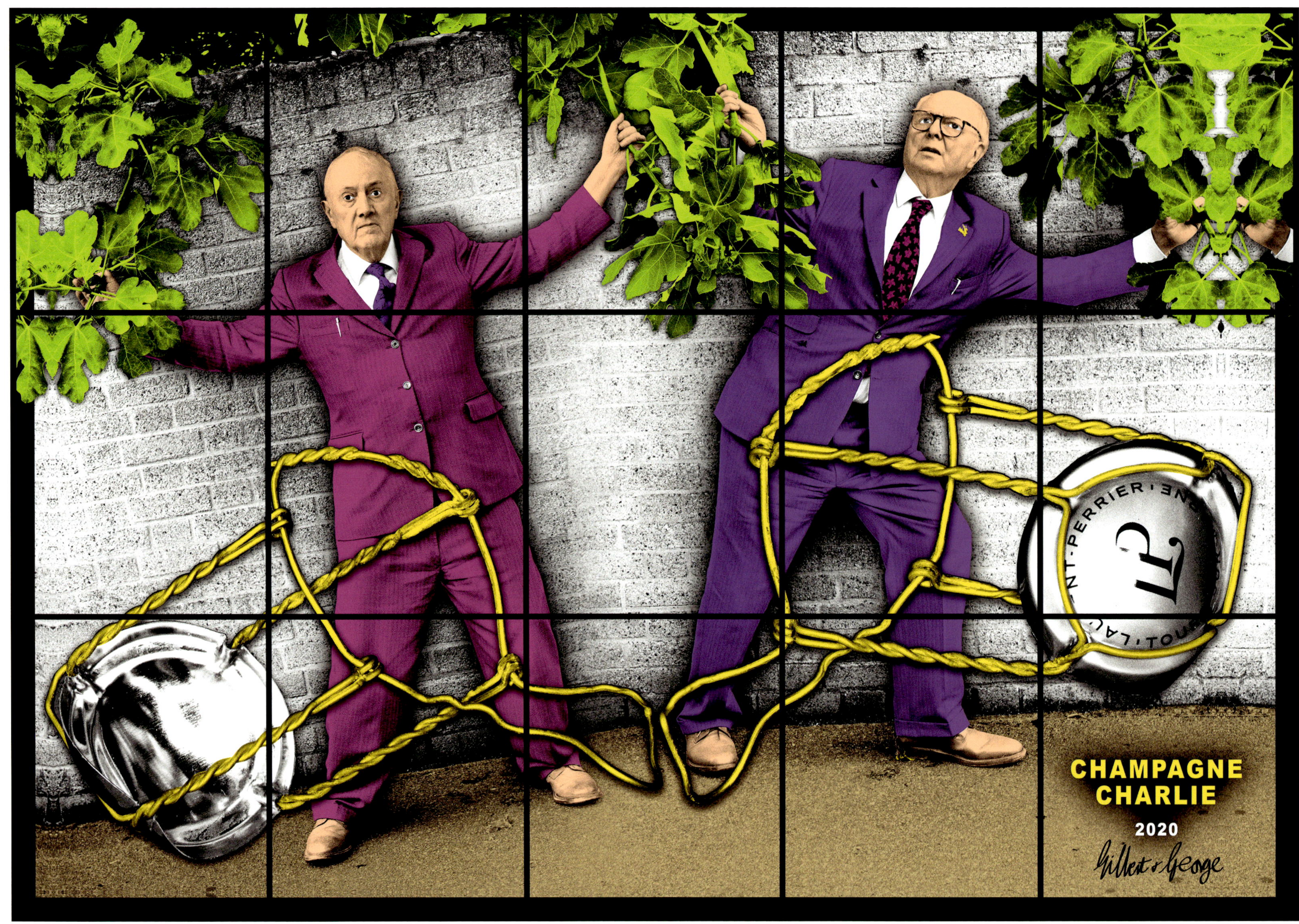

CHAMPAGNE CHARLIE. 2020. 227 x 317 cm

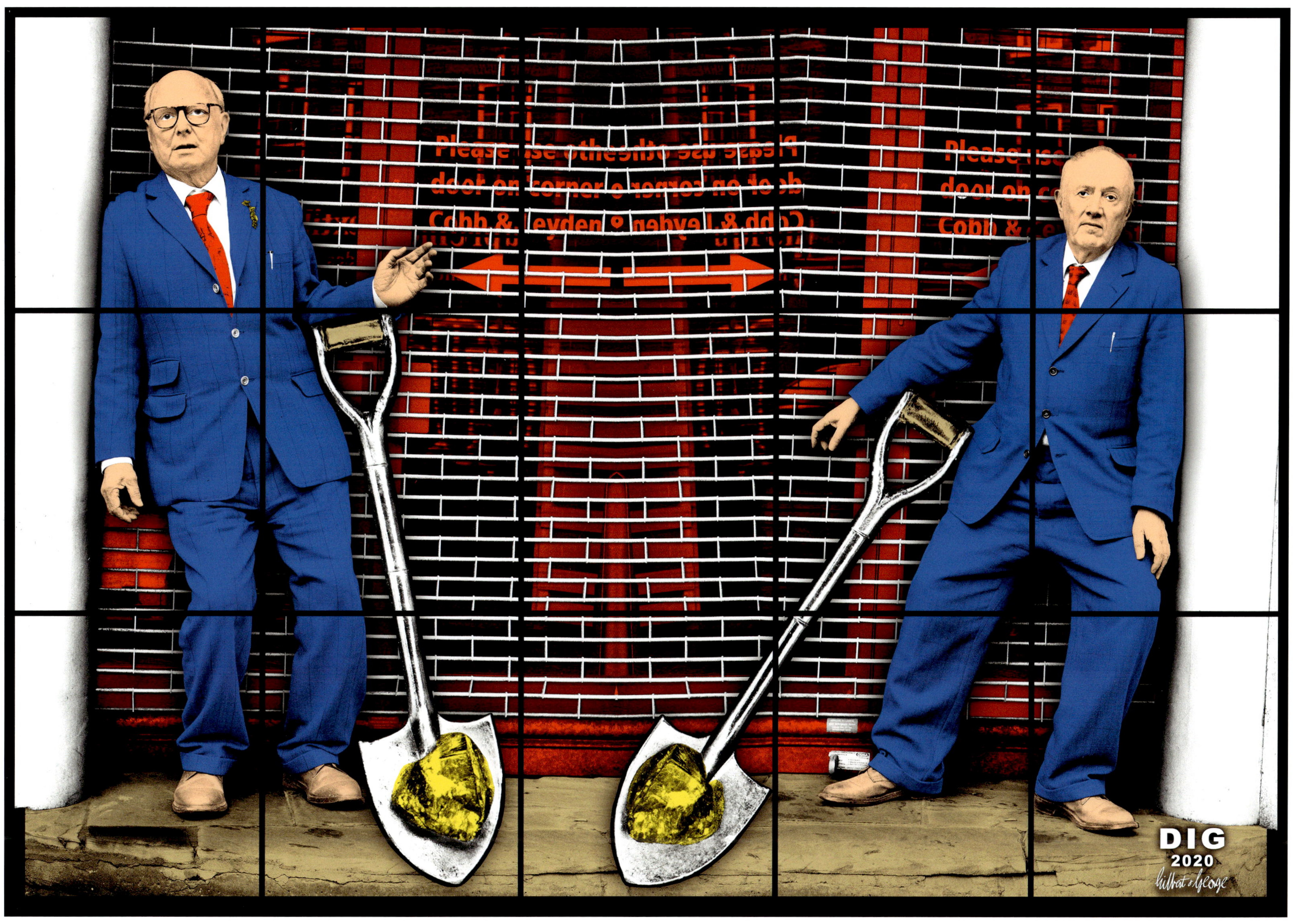

DIG. 2020. 227 x 317 cm

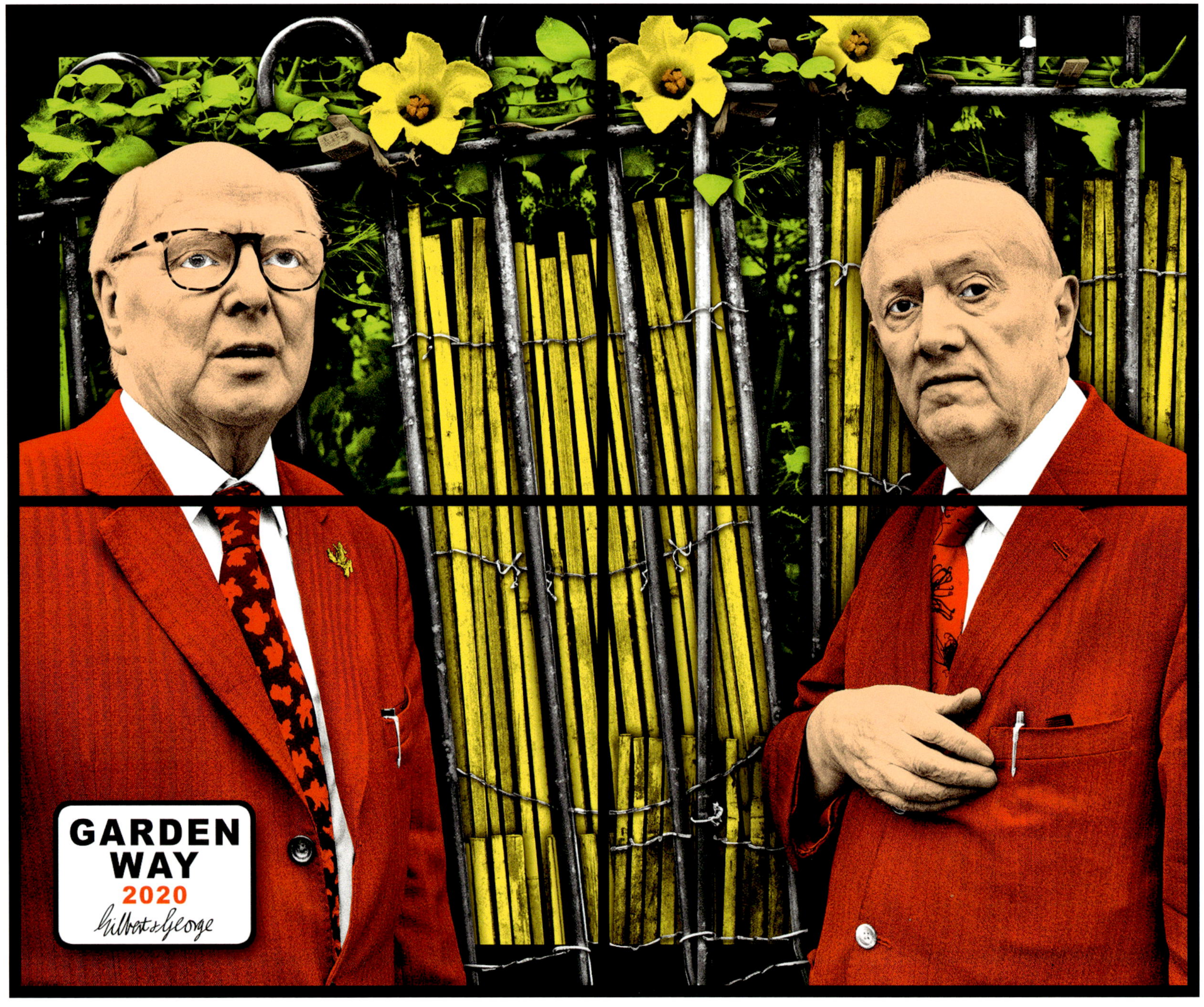

GARDEN WAY. 2020. 126 x 151 cm

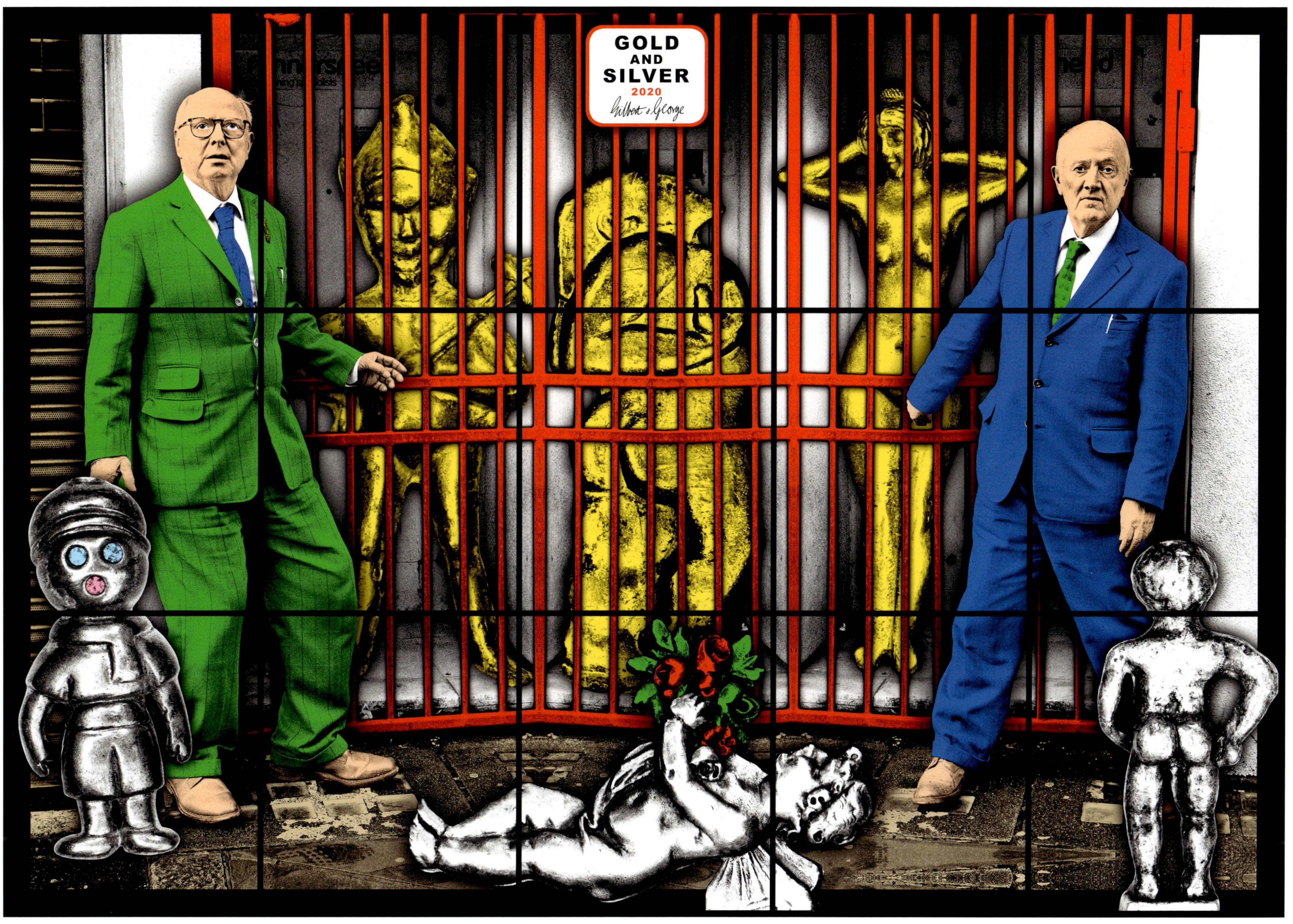

GOLD AND SILVER. 2020. 227 x 317 cm

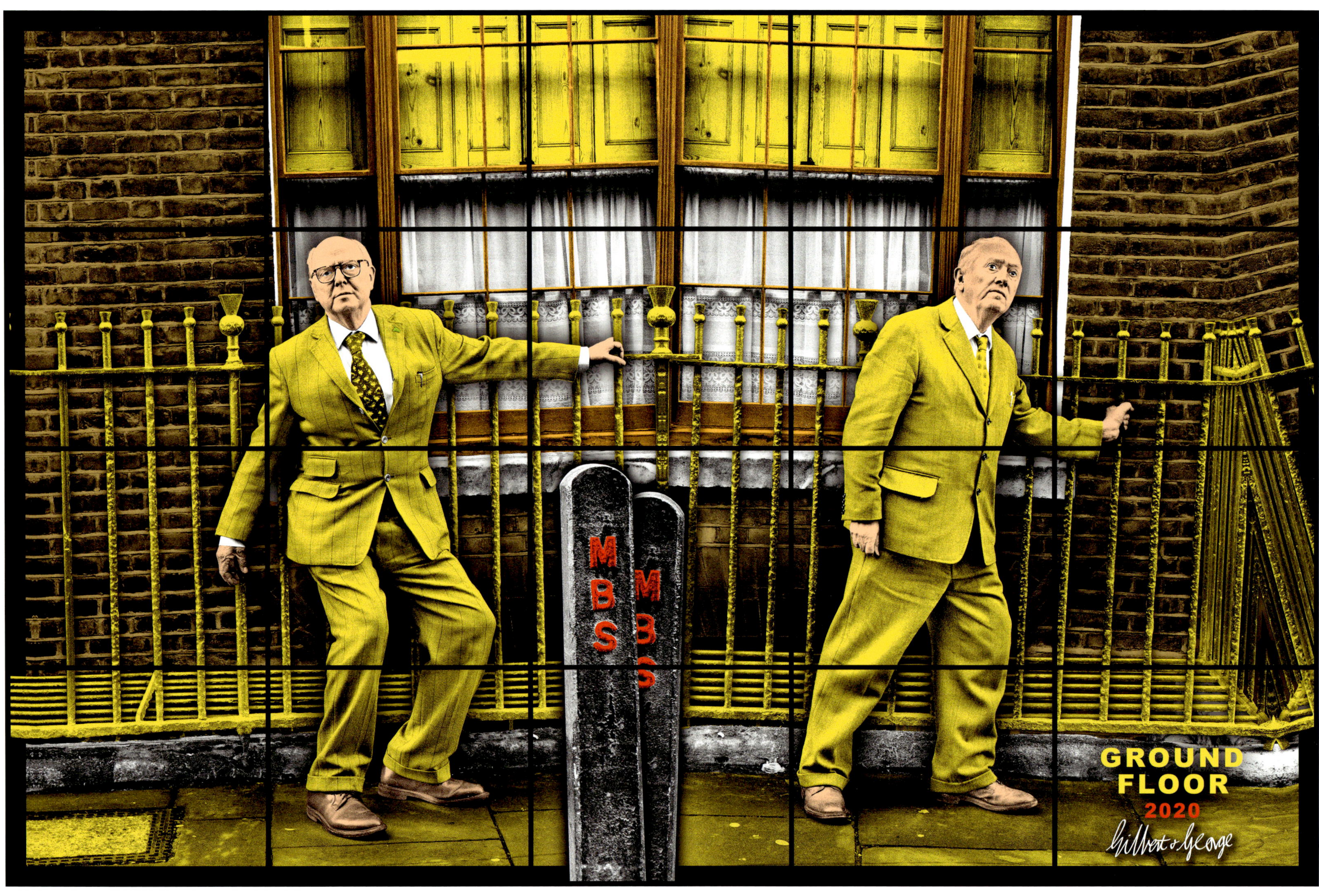

GROUND FLOOR. 2020. 302 x 377 cm

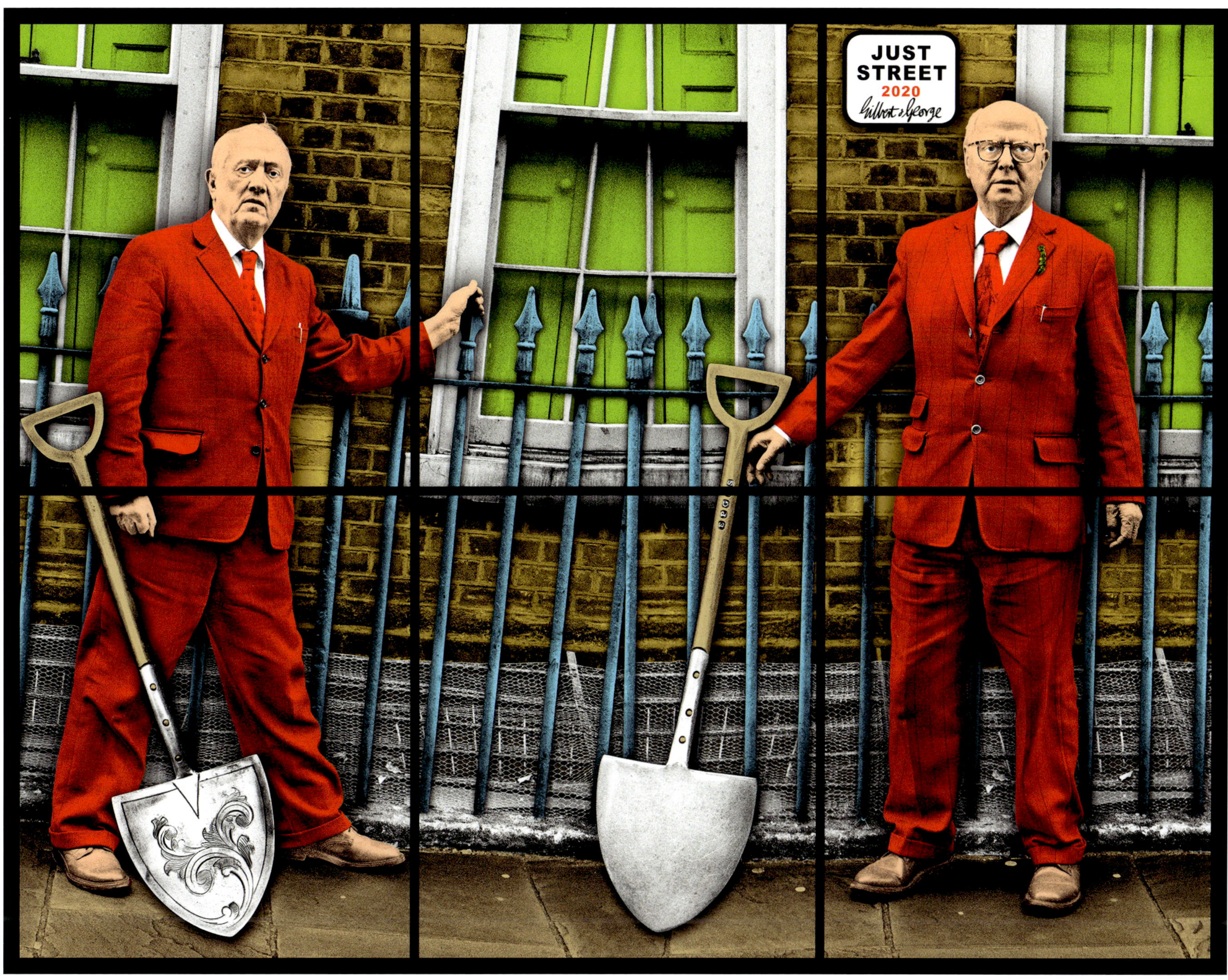

JUST STREET. 2020. 151 x 191 cm

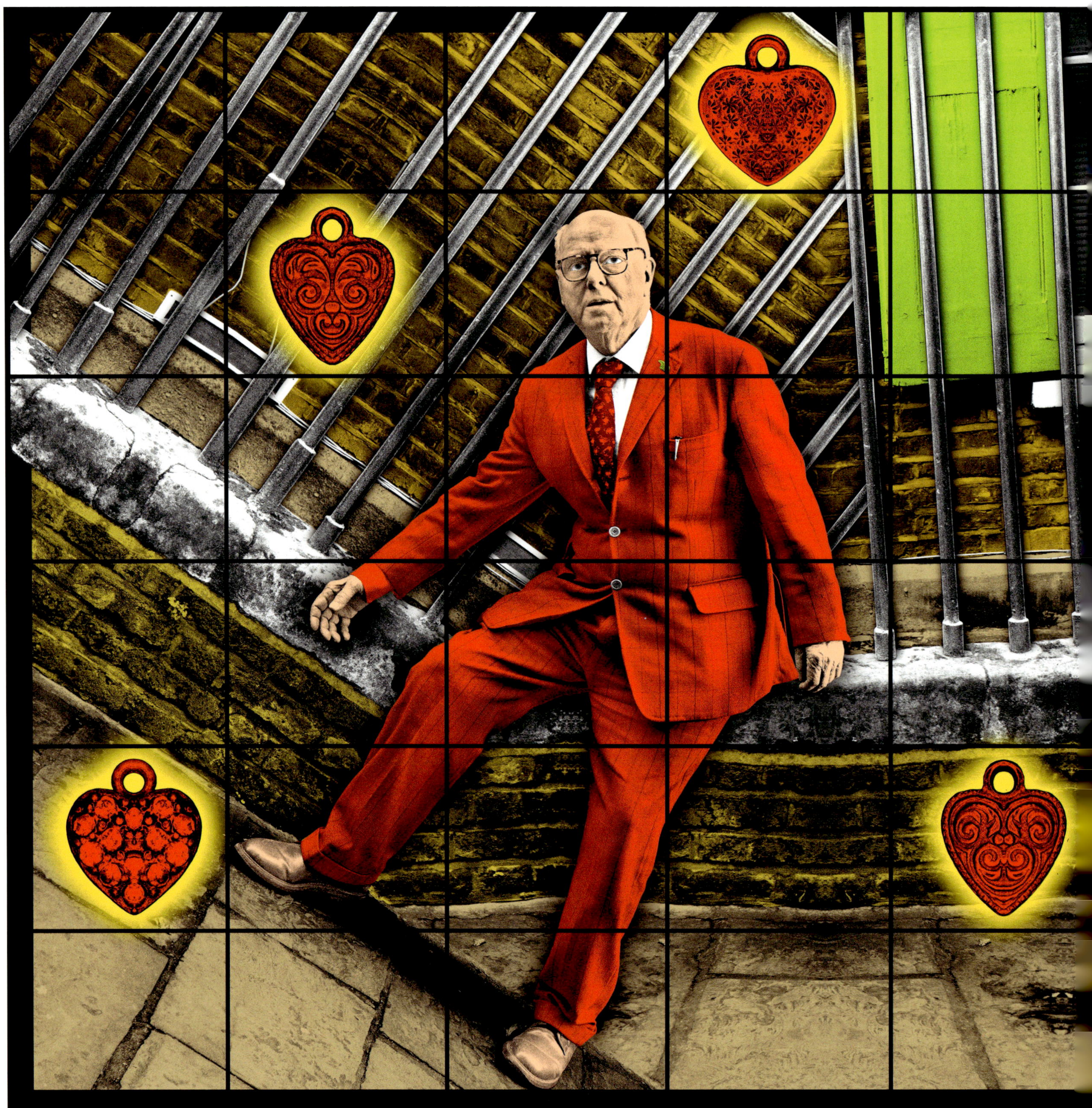

HEART LANE.
2020.
381 x 755 cm

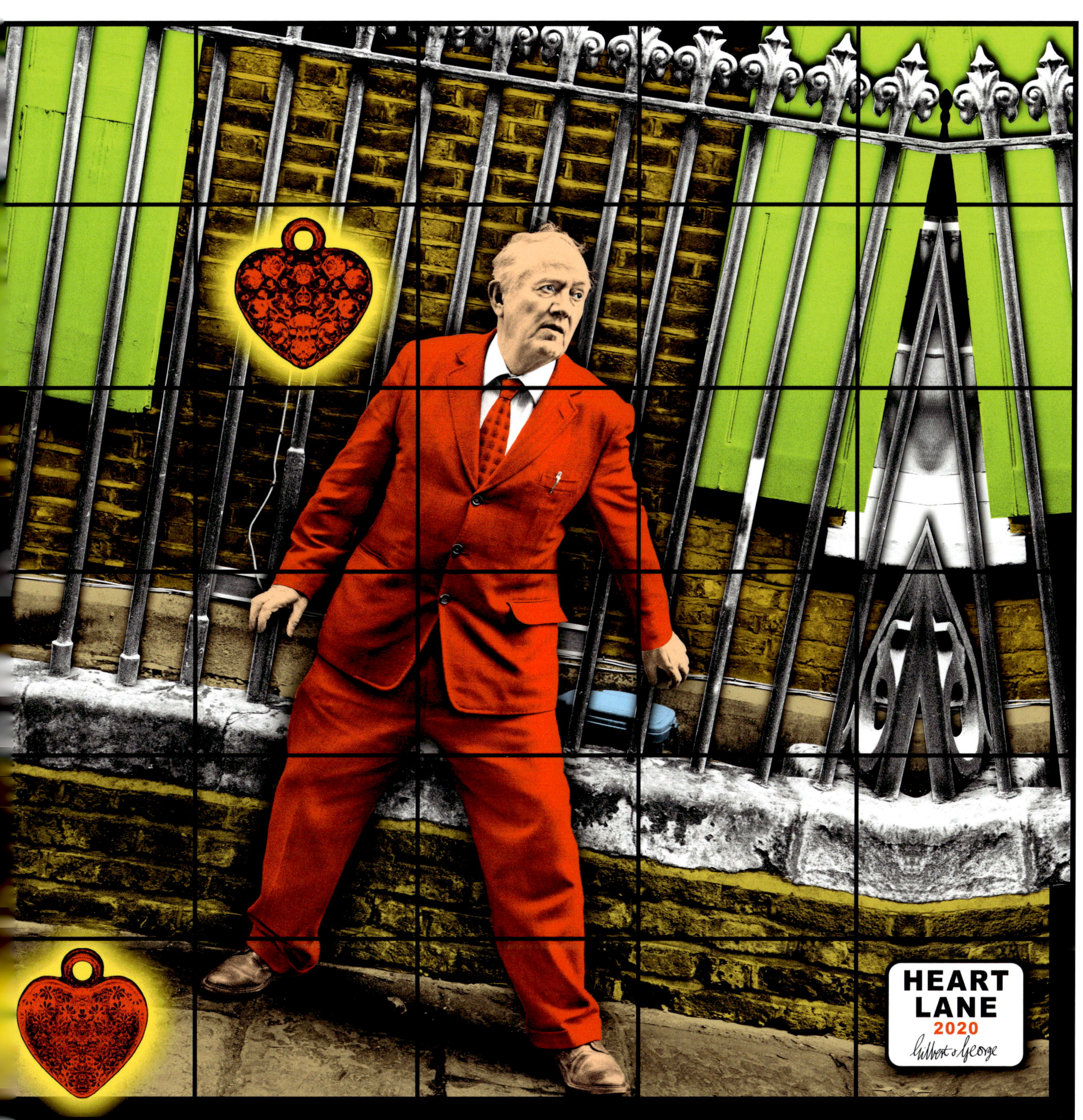
HEART
LANE
2020
Gilbert & George

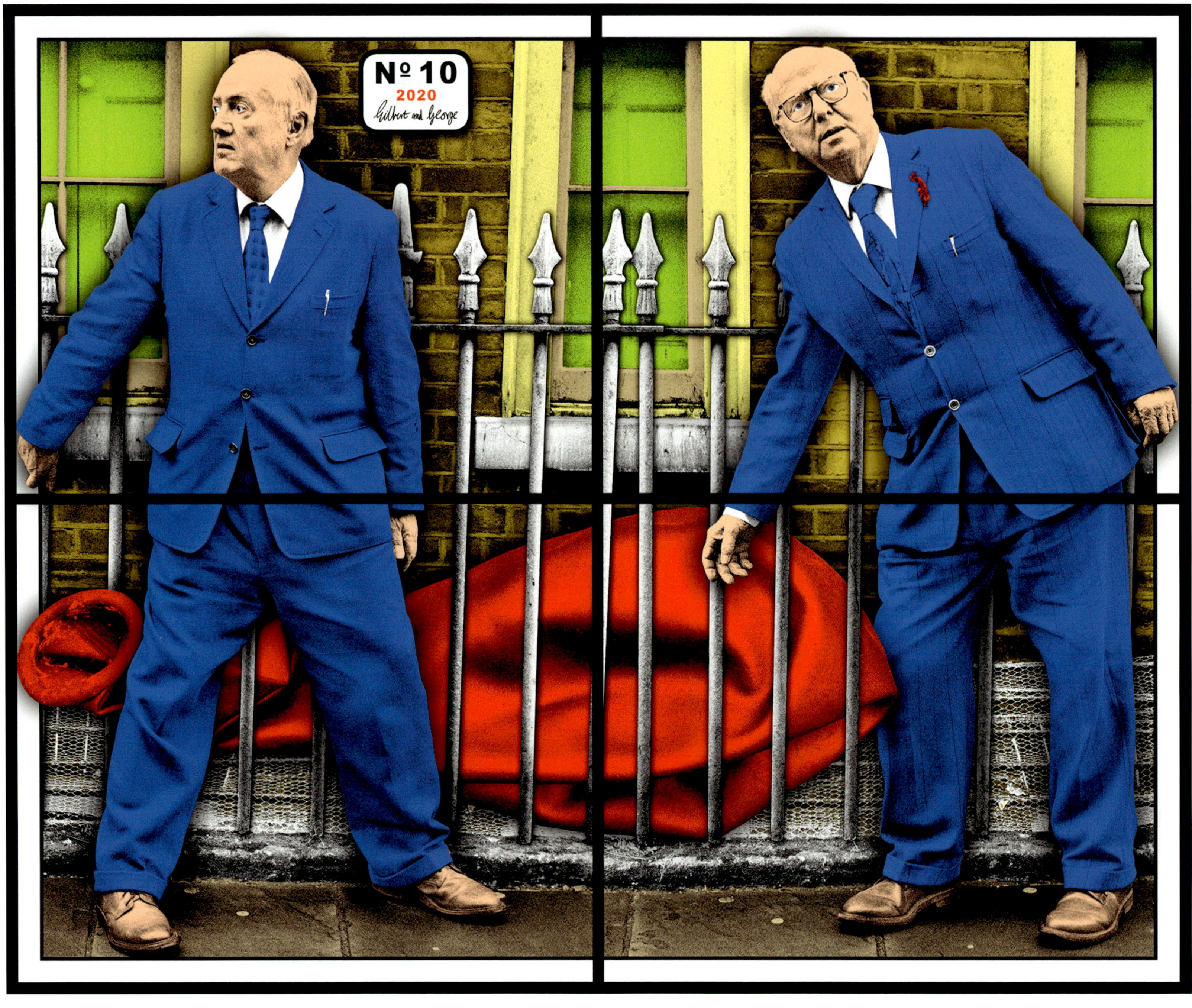

Nº 10. 2020. 127 x 151 cm

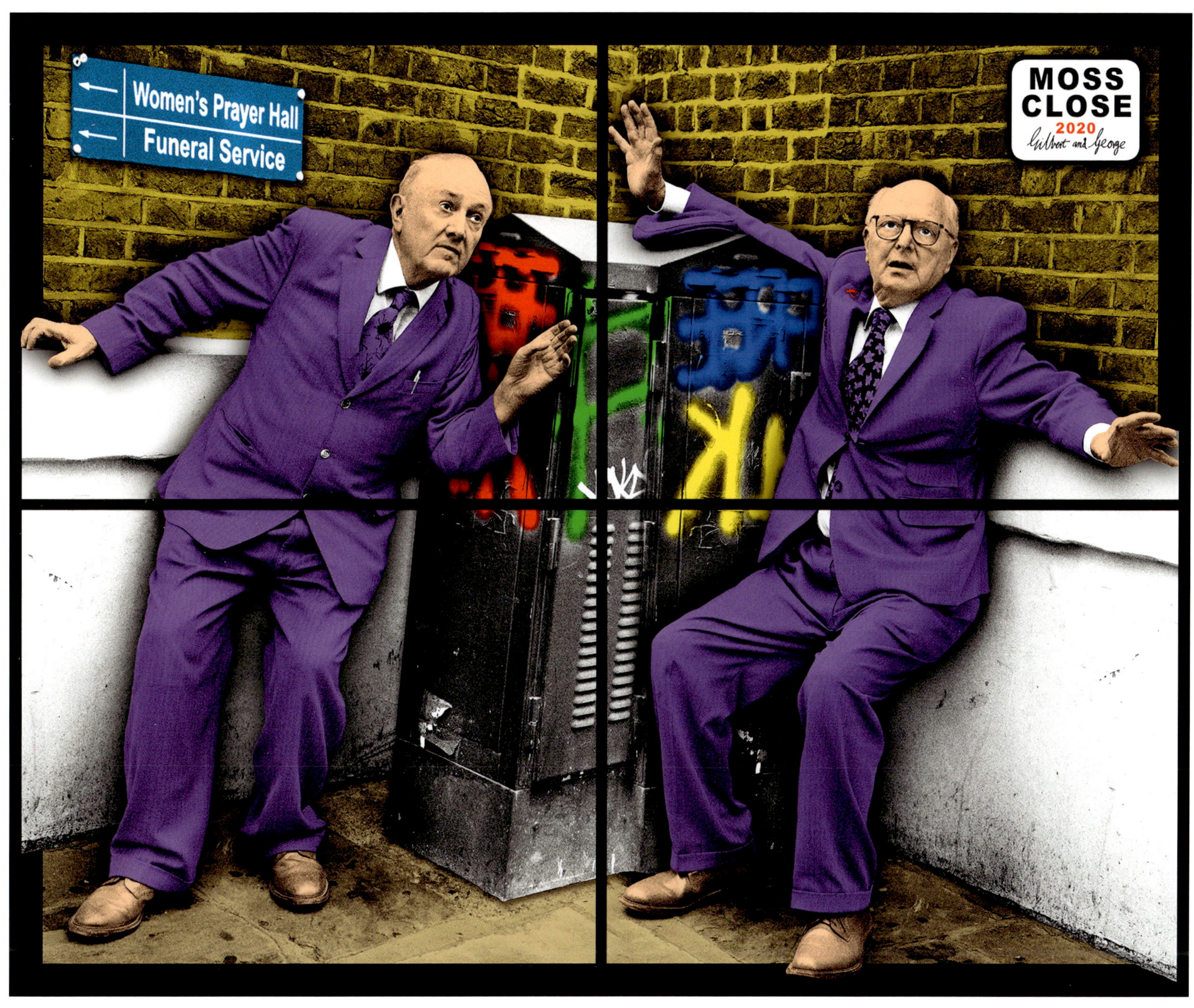

MOSS CLOSE. 2020. 127 x 151 cm

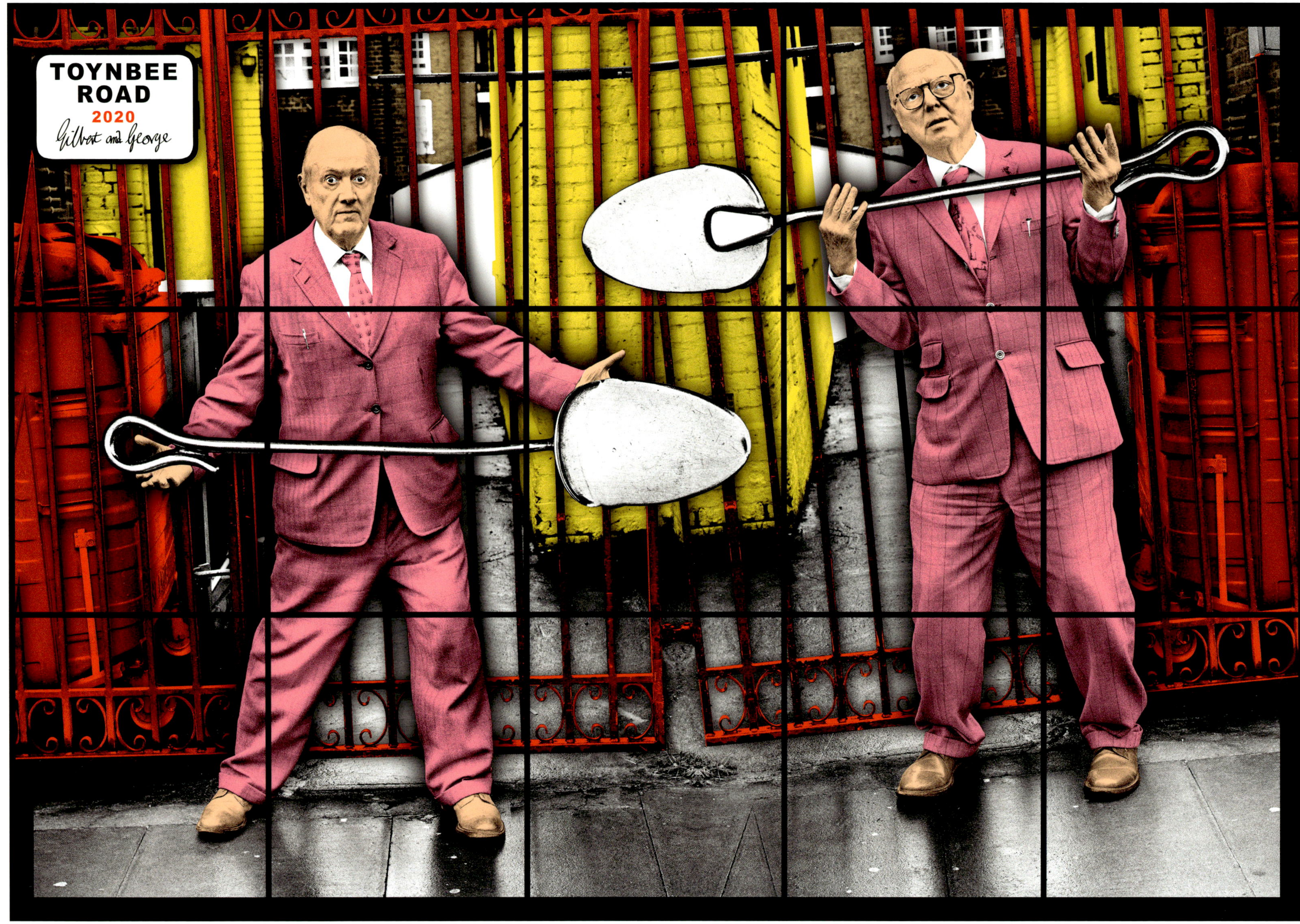

TOYNBEE ROAD. 2020. 227 x 317 cm

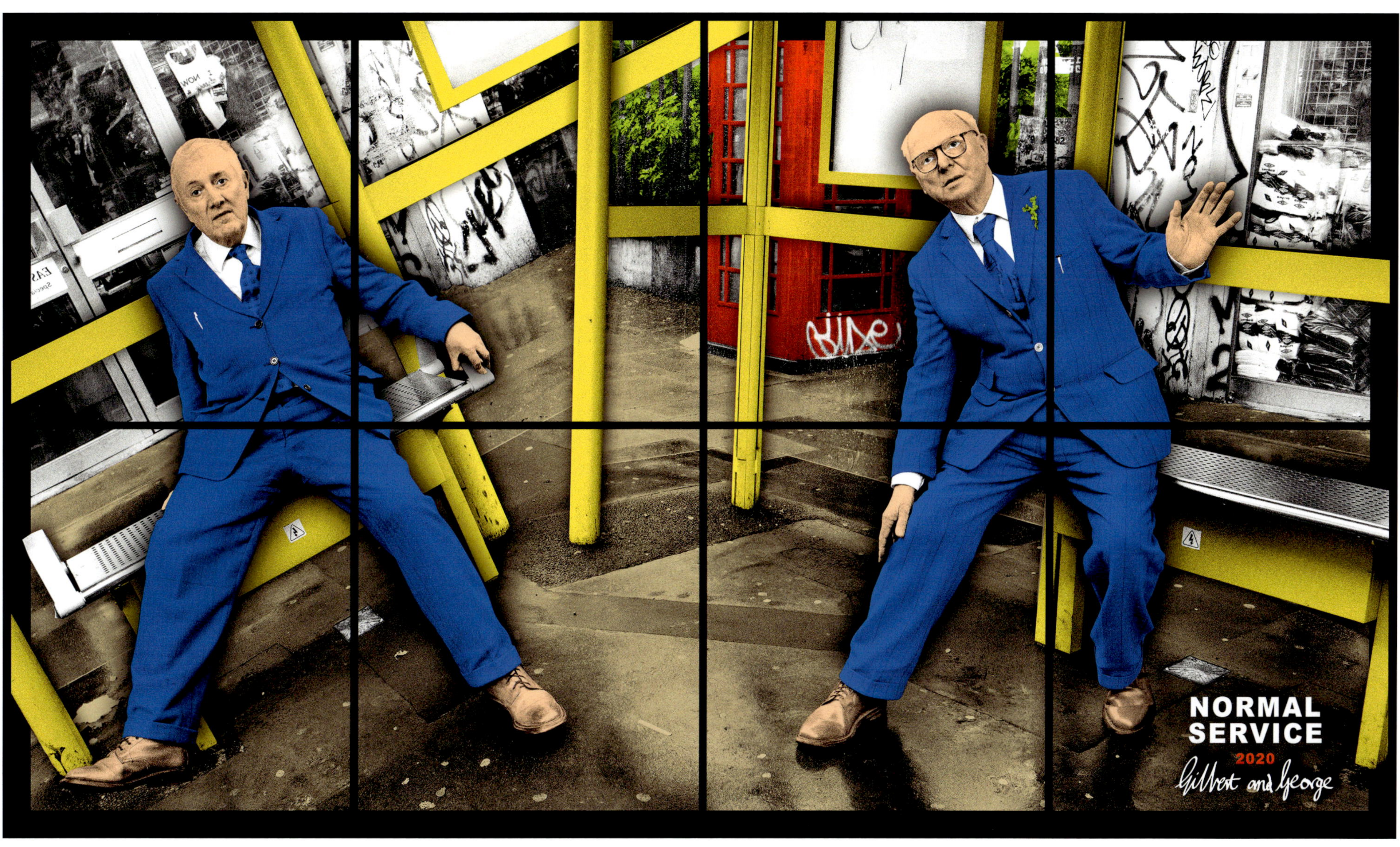

NORMAL SERVICE. 2020. 151 x 254 cm

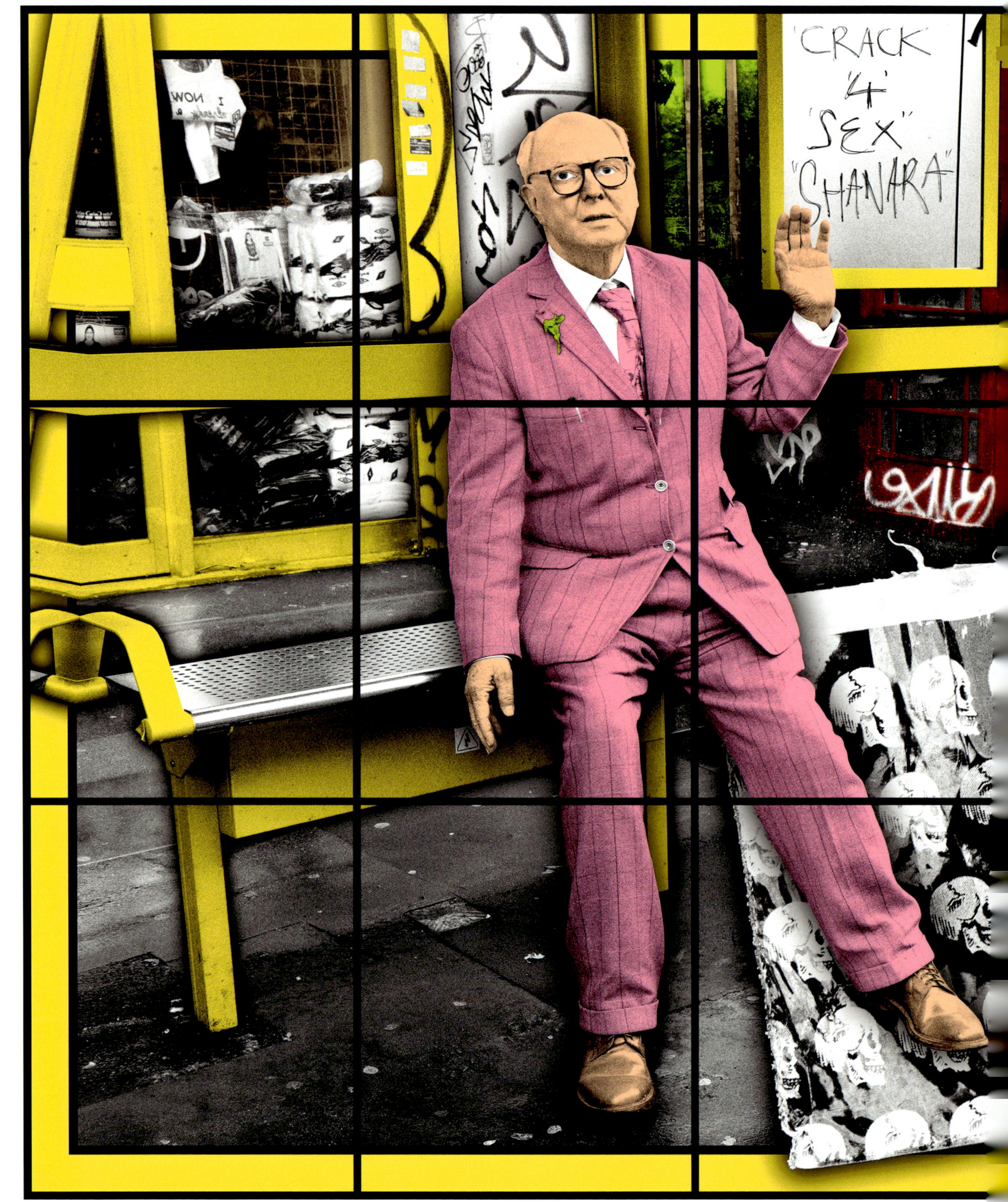
'CRACK'
'4'
'SEX'
'SHANARA'

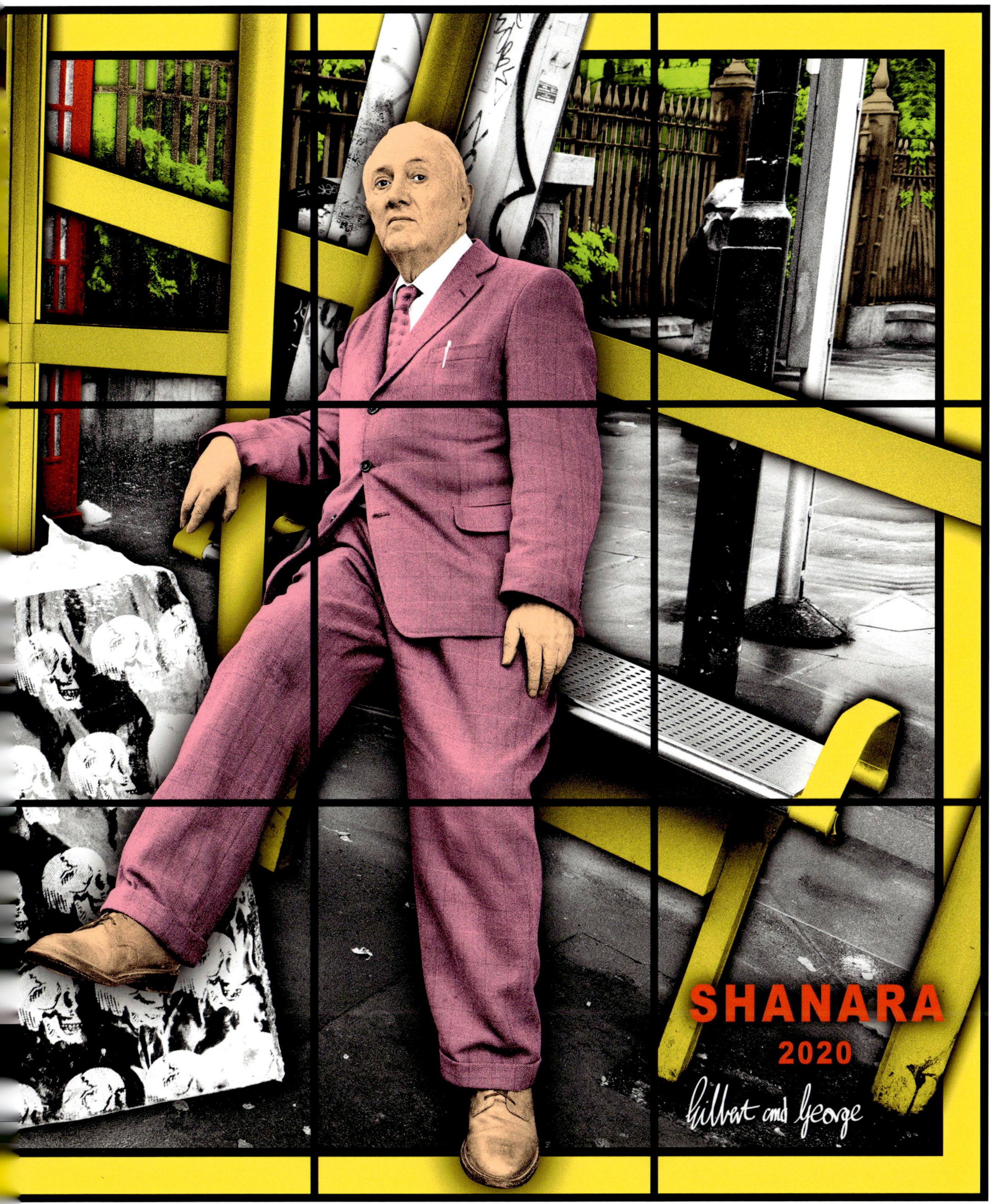

SHANARA. 2020. 227 x 381 cm

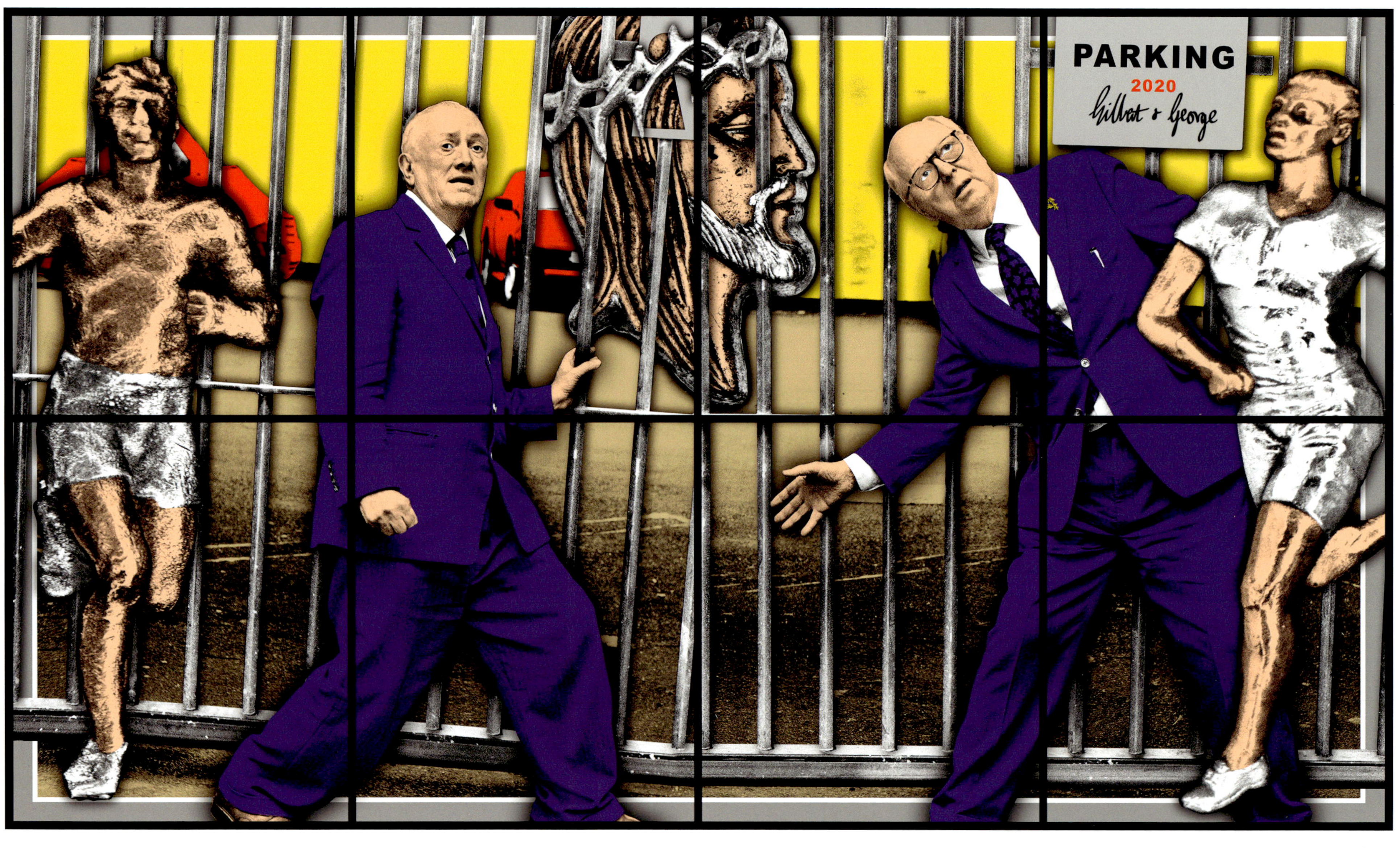

PARKING. 2020. 151 x 254 cm

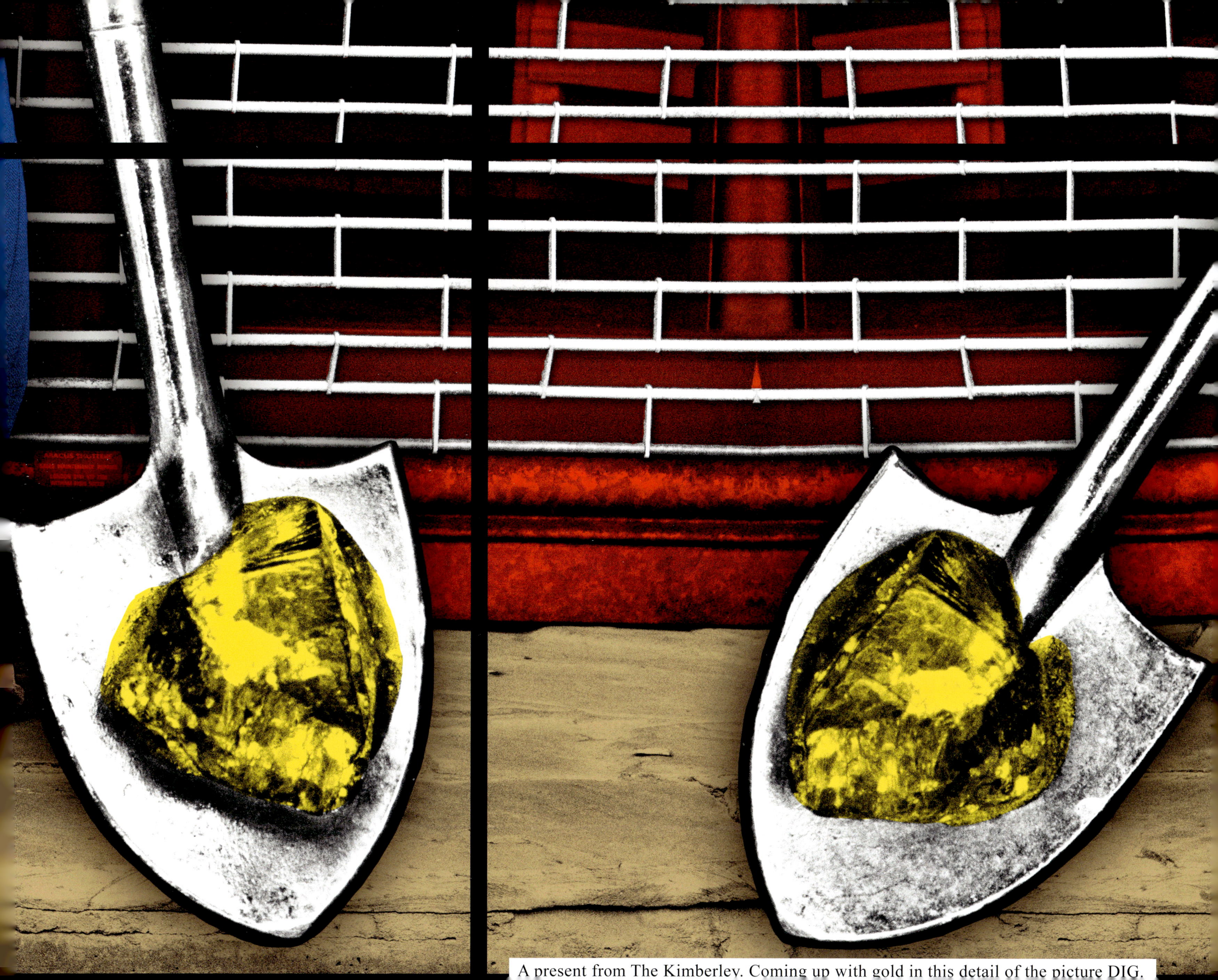

A present from The Kimberley. Coming up with gold in this detail of the picture DIG.

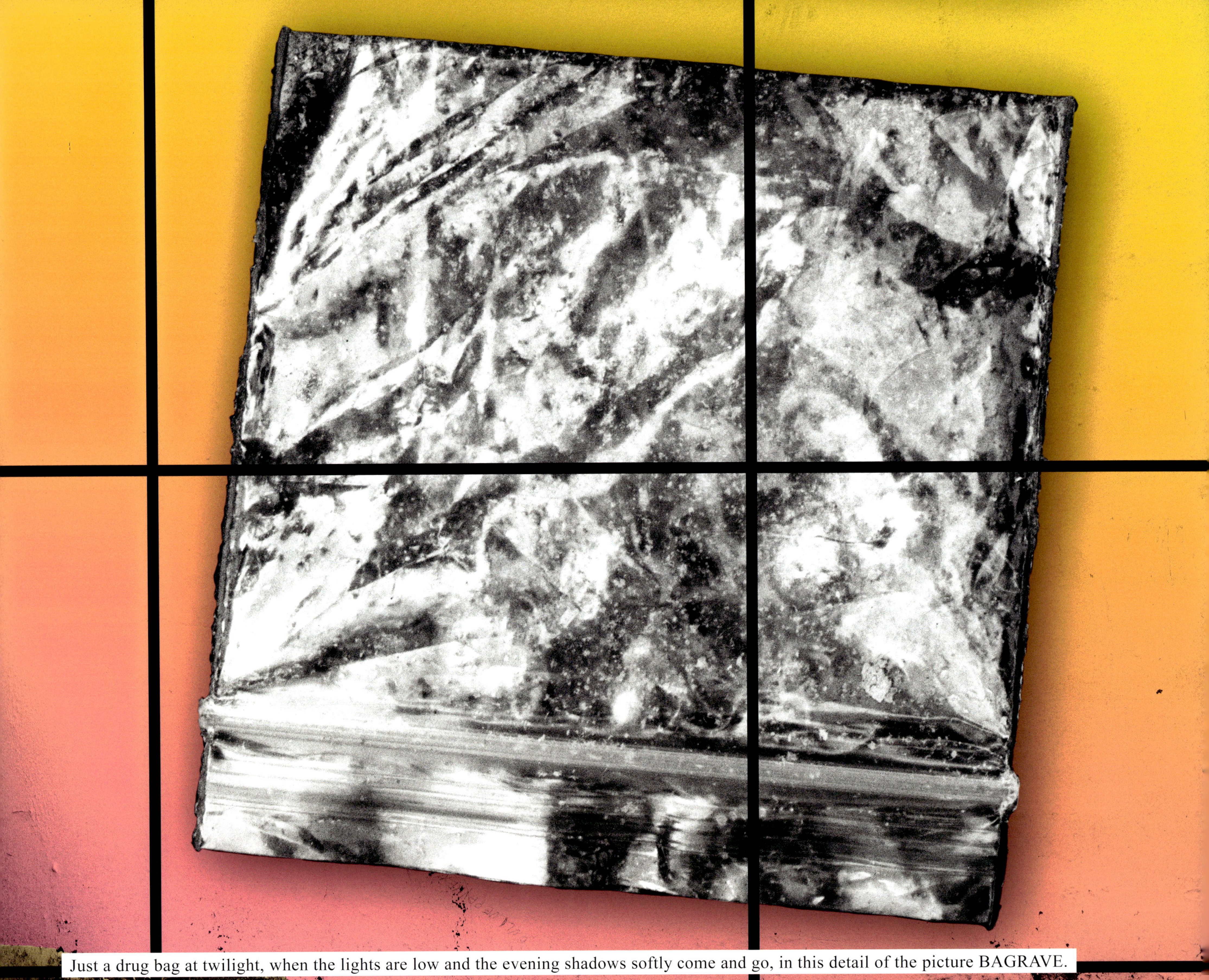

Just a drug bag at twilight, when the lights are low and the evening shadows softly come and go, in this detail of the picture BAGRAVE.

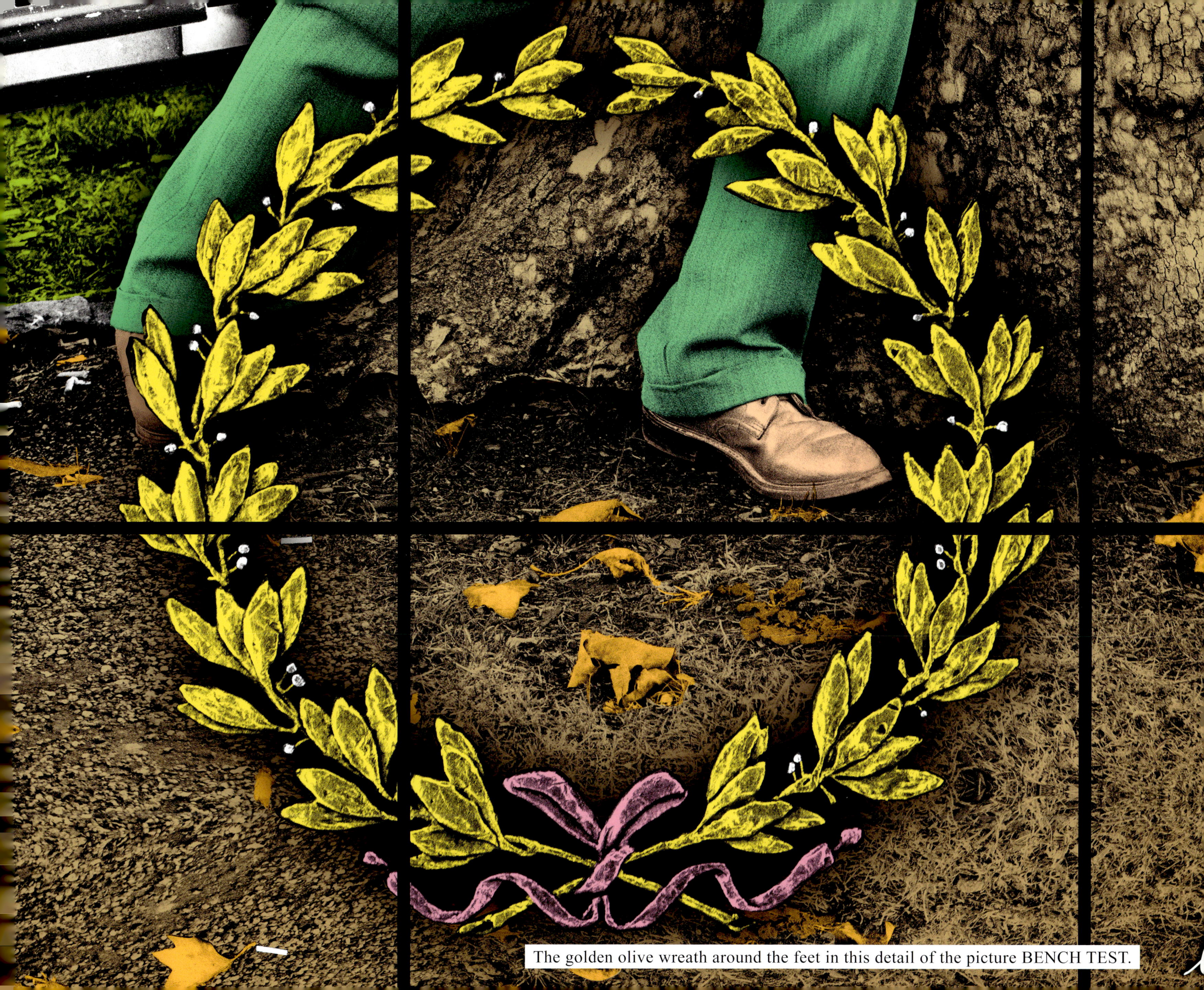

The golden olive wreath around the feet in this detail of the picture BENCH TEST.

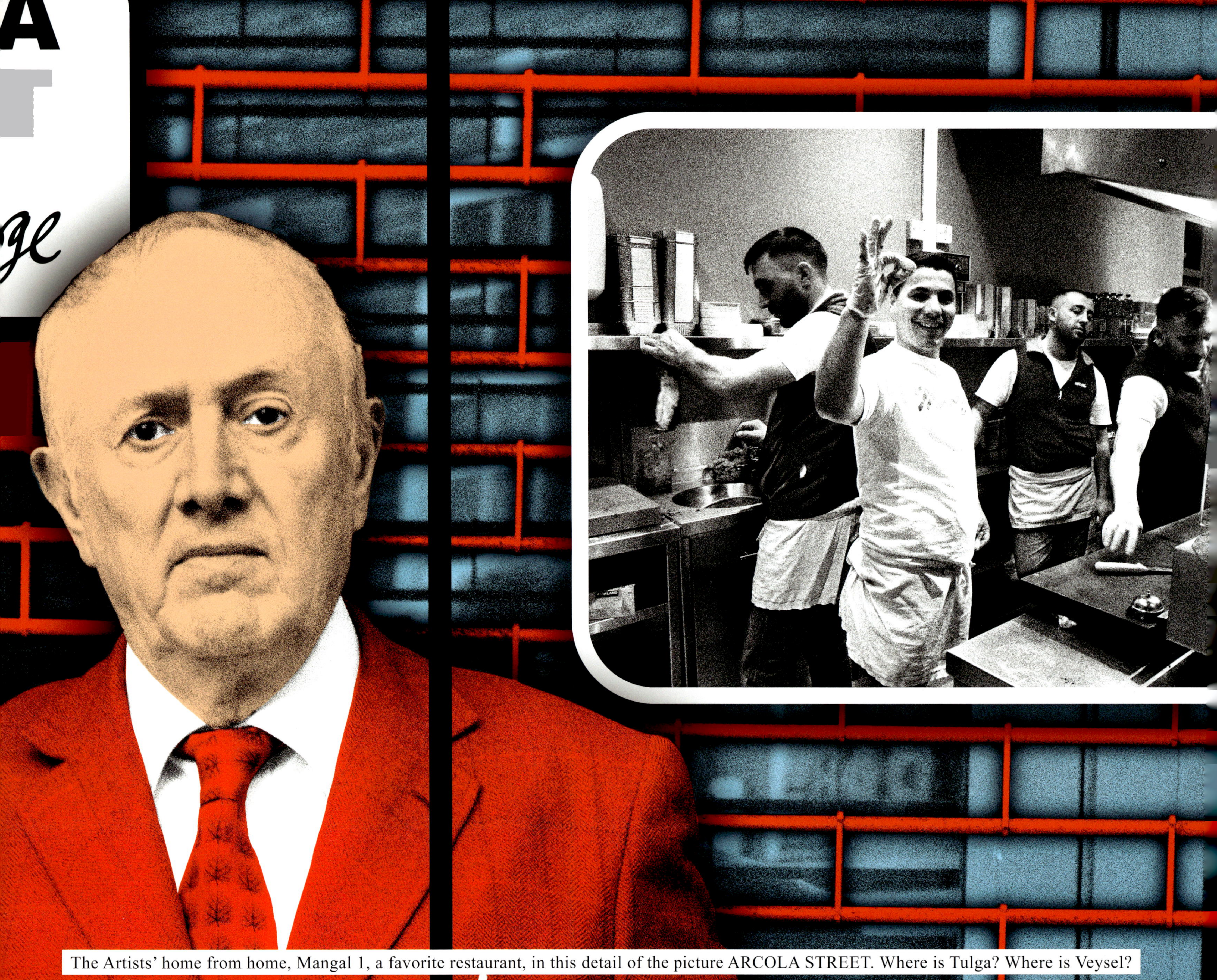

The Artists' home from home, Mangal 1, a favorite restaurant, in this detail of the picture ARCOLA STREET. Where is Tulga? Where is Veysel?

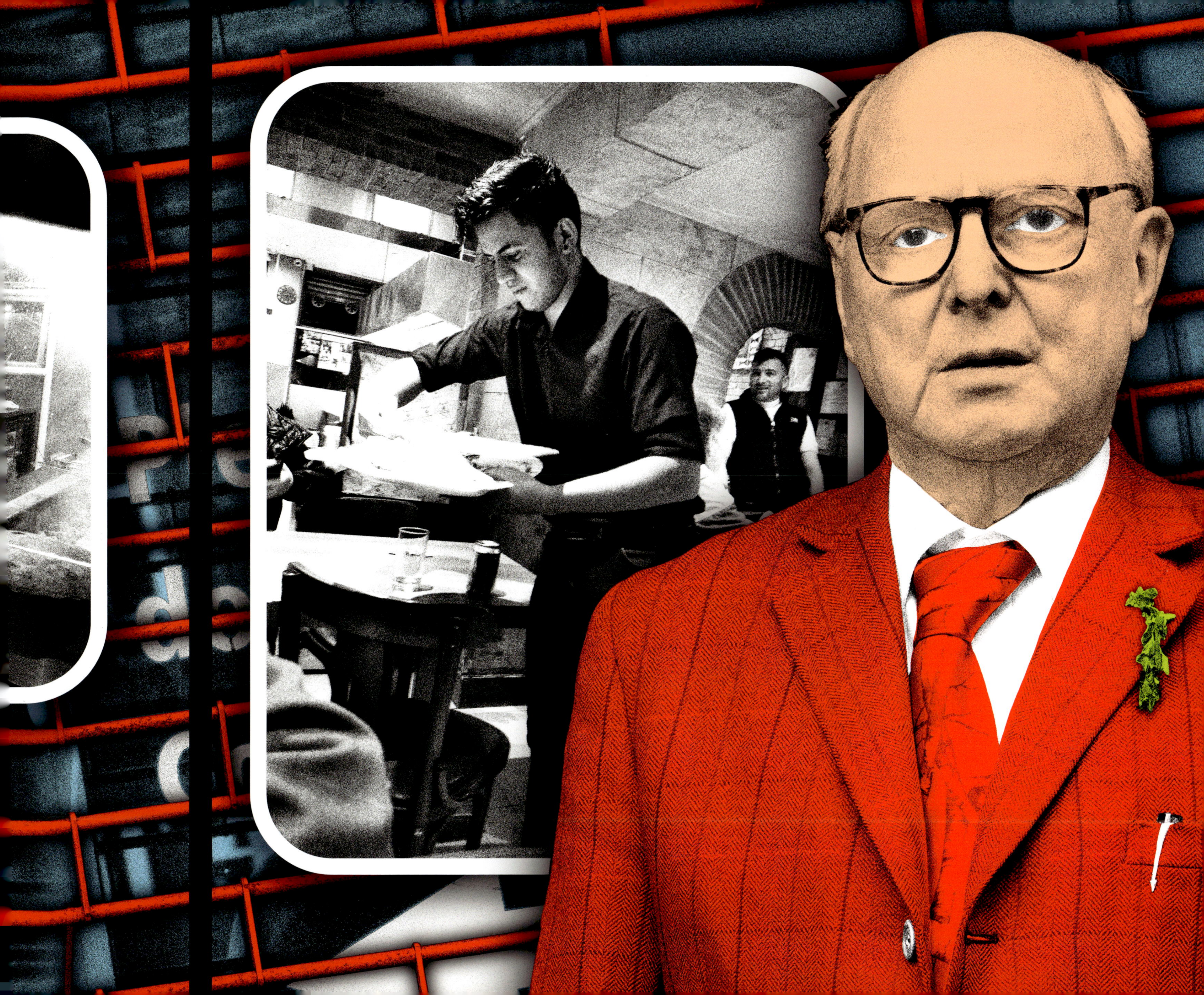

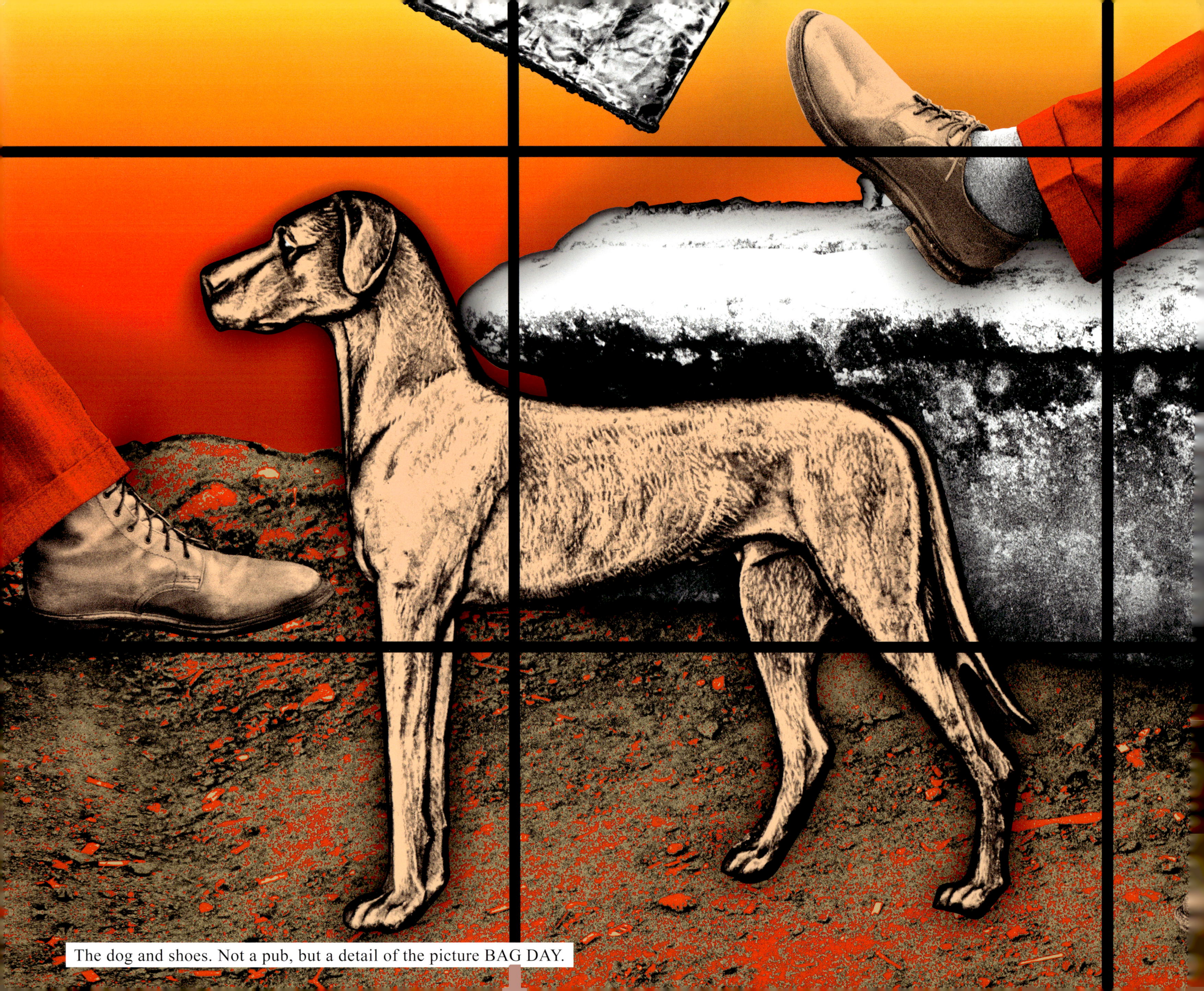

The dog and shoes. Not a pub, but a detail of the picture BAG DAY.

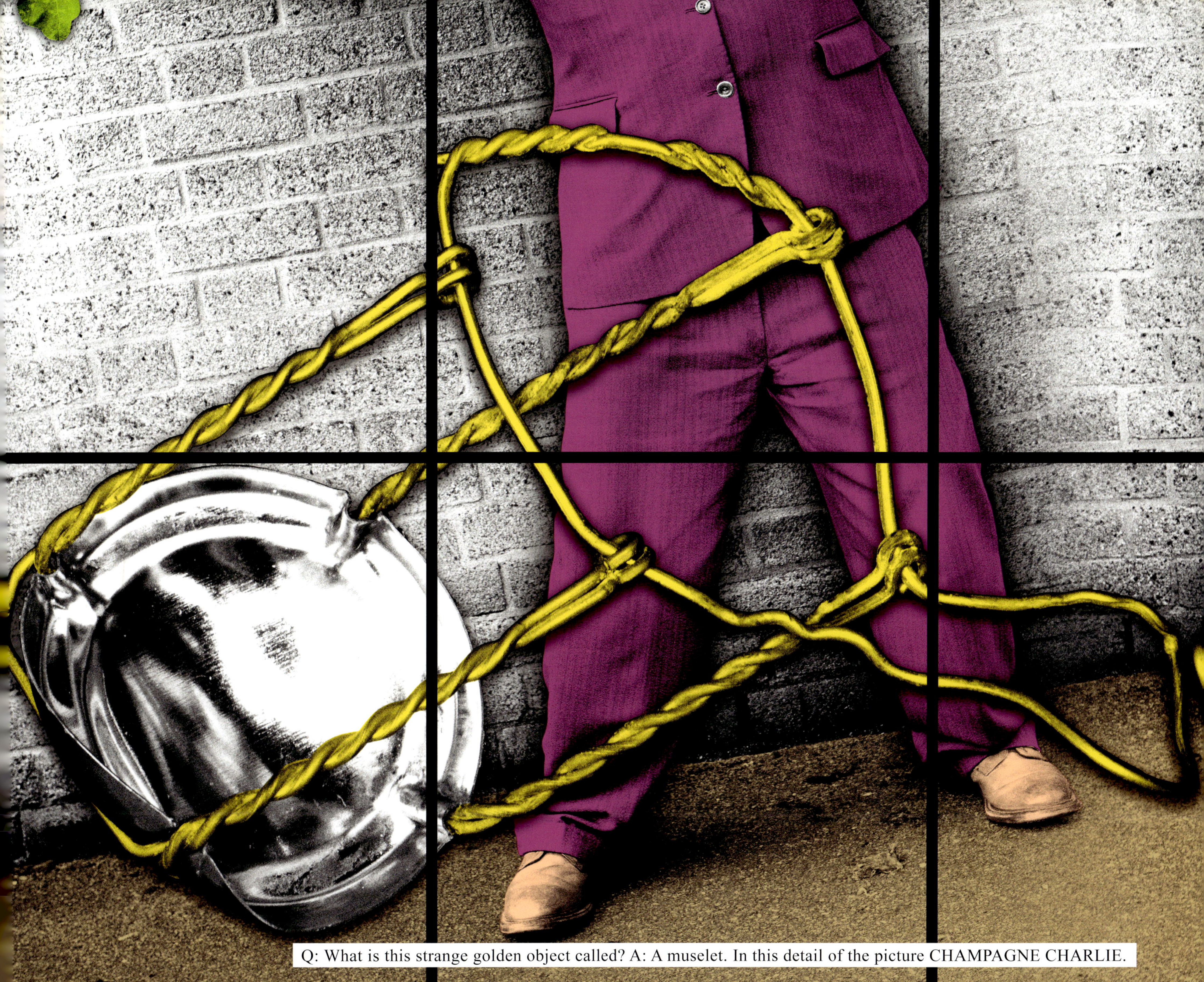

Q: What is this strange golden object called? A: A muselet. In this detail of the picture CHAMPAGNE CHARLIE.

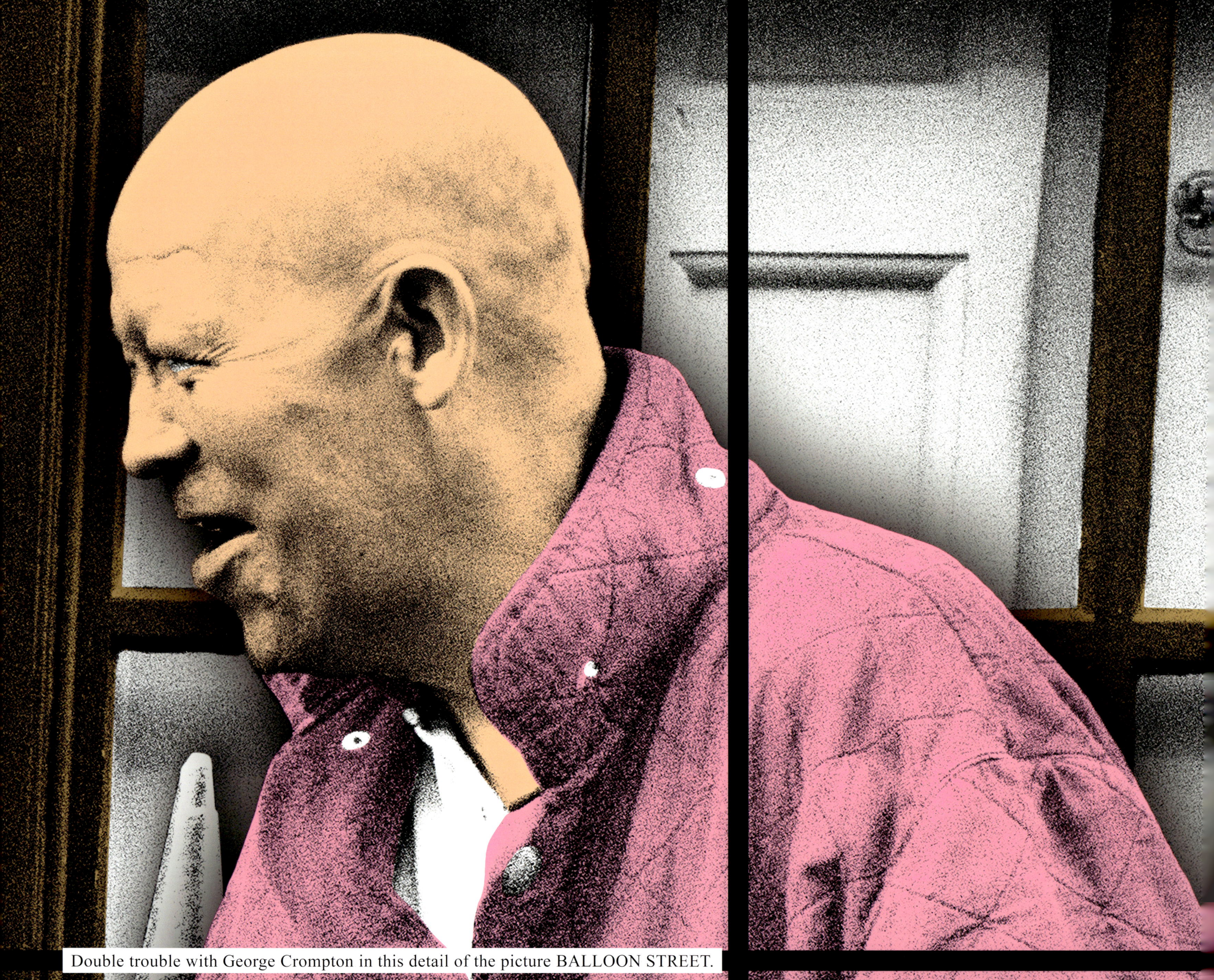
Double trouble with George Crompton in this detail of the picture BALLOON STREET.

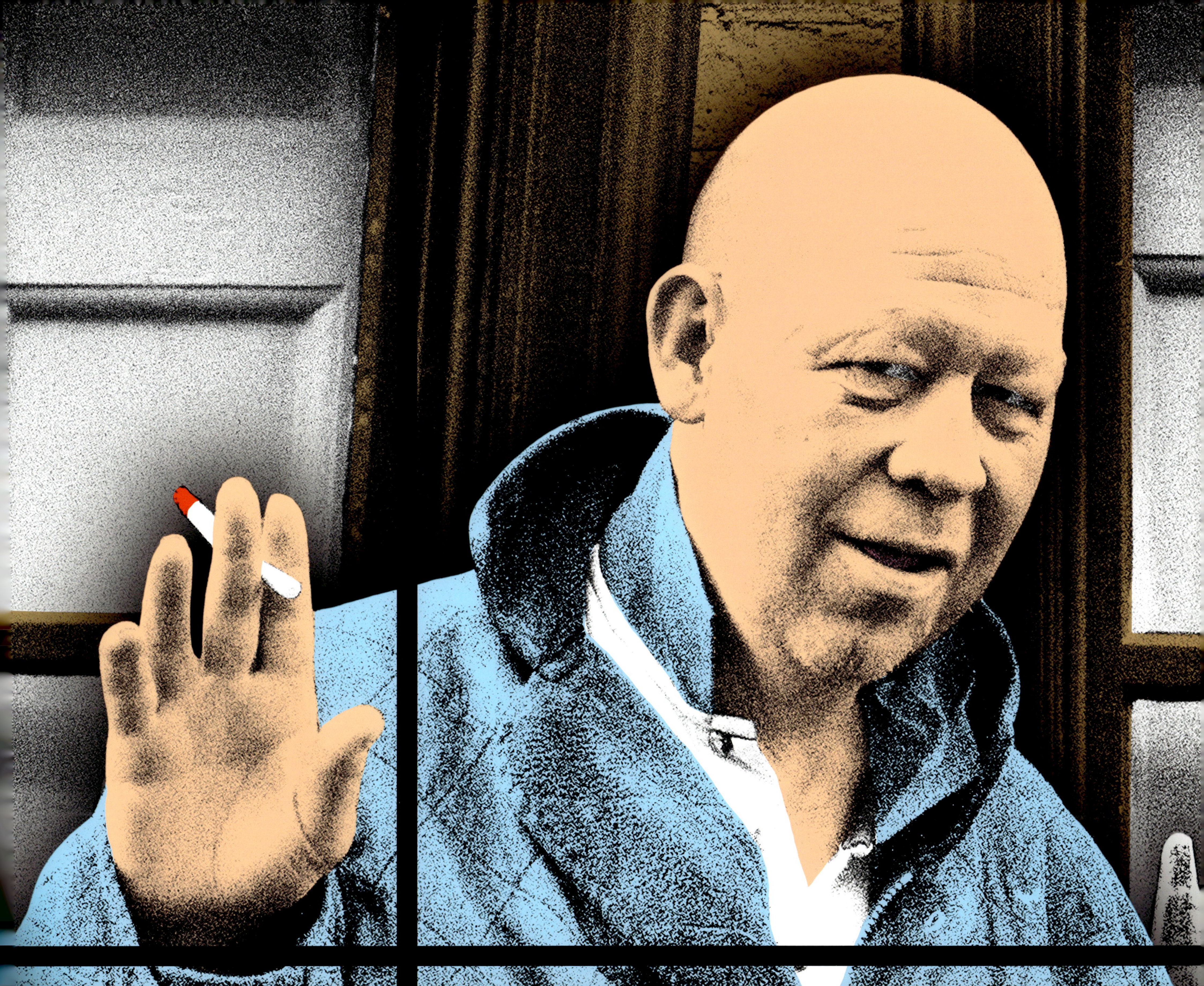

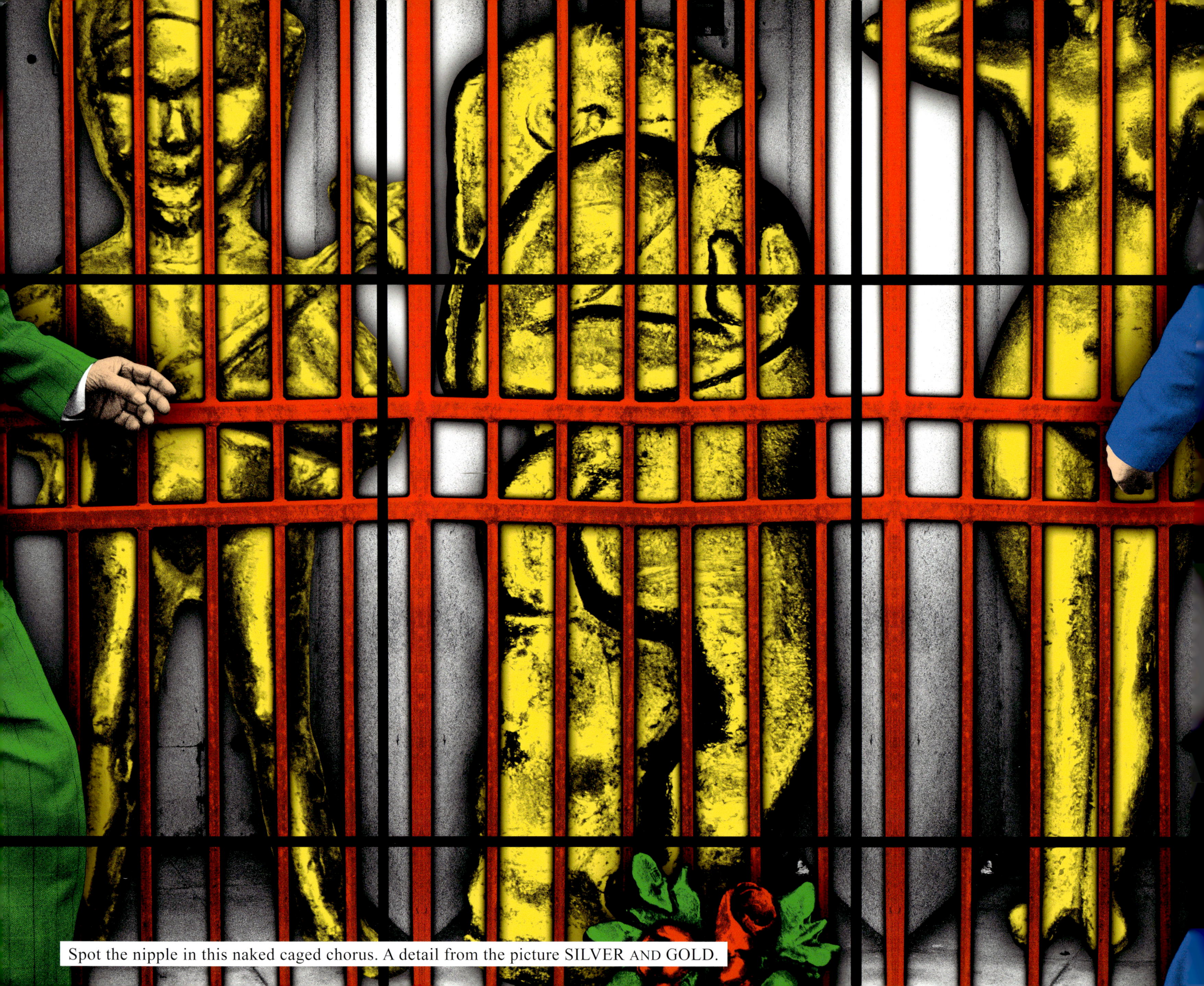

Spot the nipple in this naked caged chorus. A detail from the picture SILVER AND GOLD.

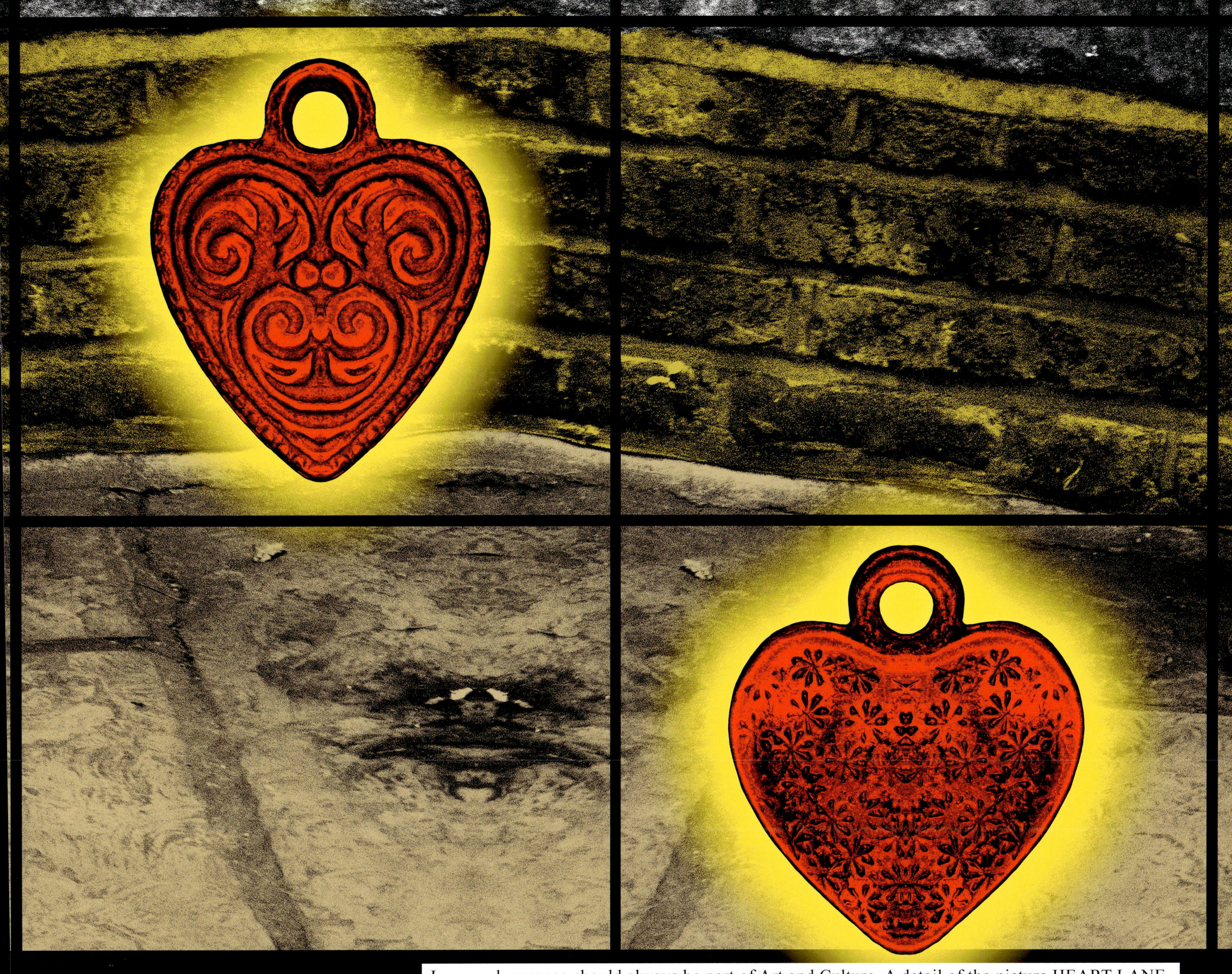

Love and romance should always be part of Art and Culture. A detail of the picture HEART LANE.

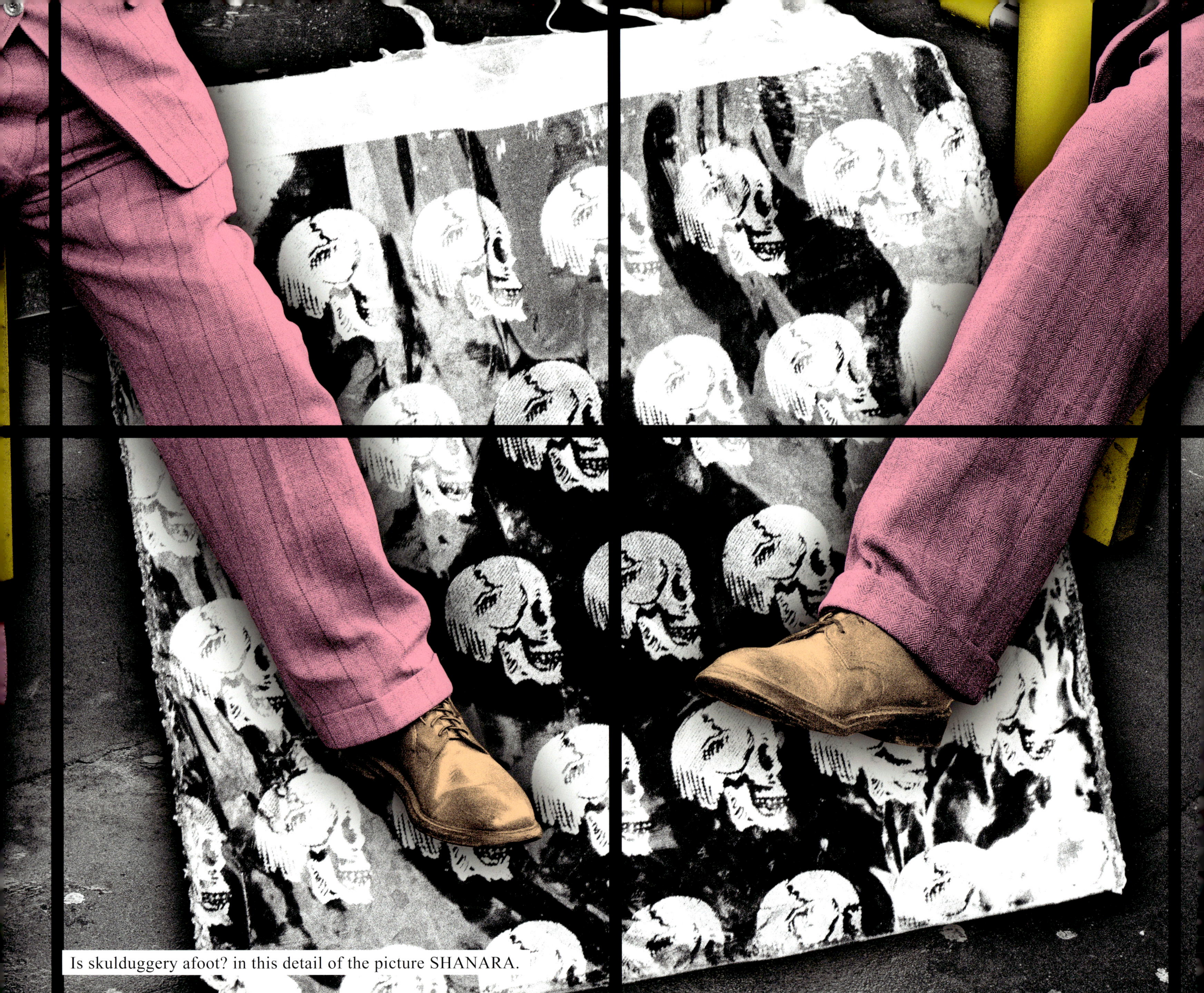

Is skulduggery afoot? in this detail of the picture SHANARA.

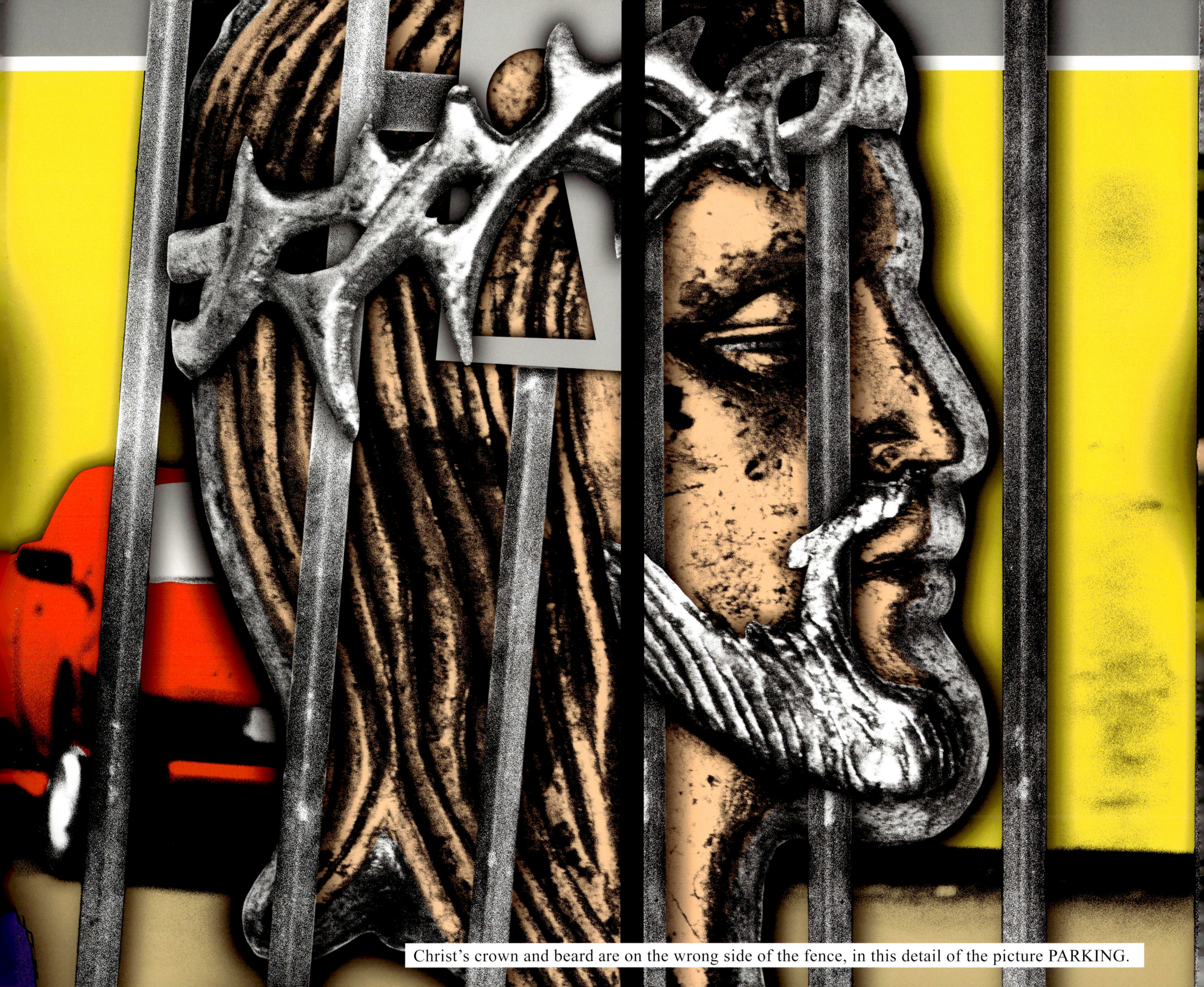

Christ's crown and beard are on the wrong side of the fence, in this detail of the picture PARKING.

MUSEUM AND PUBLIC GALLERY EXHIBITIONS 1971 to 2021

1971	THE PAINTINGS	Whitechapel Art Gallery, London
1971	THE PAINTINGS	Stedelijk Museum, Amsterdam
1971	THE PAINTINGS	Kunstverein, Düsseldorf
1972	THE PAINTINGS	Koninklijk Museum, Antwerp
1972	THE PAINTINGS	Kunstmuseum, Luzern
1973	THE SHRUBBERIES & SINGING SCULPTURE	National Gallery of NSW (J.Kaldor proj.), Sydney
1973	THE SHRUBBERIES & SINGING SCULPTURE	National Gallery (J.Kaldor proj.), Melbourne
1976	THE GENERAL JUNGLE	Albright-Knox Gallery, Buffalo
1980	PHOTO-PIECES 1971 – 1980	Van Abbemuseum, Eindhoven
1981	PHOTO-PIECES 1971 – 1980	Kunsthalle, Düsseldorf
1981	PHOTO-PIECES 1971 – 1980	Kunsthalle, Bern
1981	PHOTO-PIECES 1971 – 1980	Pompidou Centre, Paris
1981	PHOTO-PIECES 1971 – 1980	Whitechapel Art Gallery, London
1981	16TH BIENAL DE SAO PAULO	São Paulo
1982	NEW PHOTO-PIECES	Geward, Gent
1984	GILBERT & GEORGE	The Baltimore Museum of Art, Baltimore
1984	GILBERT & GEORGE	Contemporary Arts Museum, Houston
1984	GILBERT & GEORGE	Norton Gallery, West Palm Beach, Florida
1985	GILBERT & GEORGE	Milwaukee Art Museum, Milwaukee
1985	GILBERT & GEORGE	Guggenheim Museum, New York
1986	PICTURES 1982 – 1985	CAPC, Bordeaux
1986	CHARCOAL ON PAPER SCULPTURES 1970 – 1974	CAPC, Bordeaux
1986	THE PAINTINGS 1971	The Fruitmarket, Edinburgh
1986	PICTURES 1982 – 1985	Kunsthalle, Basel
1986	PICTURES 1982 – 1985	Palais des Beaux-Arts, Brussels
1987	PICTURES 1982 – 1985	Palacio de Velasquez, Madrid
1987	PICTURES 1982 – 1985	Lenbachaus, Munich
1987	PICTURES 1982 – 1985	The Hayward Gallery, London
1987	THE 1986 PICTURES	Aldrich Museum, Ridgefield
1990	PICTURES 1983 – 88	Central House of the Artists, Moscow
1991	THE COSMOLOGICAL PICTURES	Palac Sztuki, Krakow
1991	THE COSMOLOGICAL PICTURES	Palazzo delle Esposizioni, Rome
1992	THE COSMOLOGICAL PICTURES	Kunsthalle, Zürich
1992	THE COSMOLOGICAL PICTURES	Wiener Secession, Vienna
1992	THE COSMOLOGICAL PICTURES	Ernst Múzeum, Budapest
1992	THE COSMOLOGICAL PICTURES	Haags Gemeentemusem, The Hague
1992	NEW DEMOCRATIC PICTURES	Aarhus Kunstmuseum, Aarhus
1992	THE COSMOLOGICAL PICTURES	Irish Museum of Modern Art, Dublin
1992	THE COSMOLOGICAL PICTURES	Fundació Joan Miró, Barcelona
1993	THE COSMOLOGICAL PICTURES	Tate Gallery, Liverpool
1993	THE COSMOLOGICAL PICTURES	Württembergischer Kunstverein, Stuttgart
1993	GILBERT & GEORGE CHINA EXHIBITION	National Art Gallery, Beijing
1993	GILBERT & GEORGE CHINA EXHIBITION	The Art Museum, Shanghai
1994	RETROSPECTIVE	Museo d'Arte Moderna, Lugano
1994	SHITTY NAKED HUMAN WORLD	Wolfsburg Kunstmuseum, Wolfsburg
1995	THE NAKED SHIT PICTURES	South London Gallery, London
1996	THE NAKED SHIT PICTURES	Stedelijk Museum, Amsterdam
1996	GILBERT & GEORGE RETROSPECTIVE	Galleria d'Arte Moderna, Bologna
1997	GILBERT & GEORGE RETROSPECTIVE	Sezon Museum, Tokyo
1997	PICTURES 1991 – 1996	Magasin 3, Stockholm
1997	GILBERT & GEORGE RETROSPECTIVE	Musée d'Art Moderne de la Ville, Paris

1998	NEW TESTAMENTAL PICTURES	Museo di Capodimonte, Naples
1999	GILBERT & GEORGE 1970 – 1988	Astrup Fearnley Museet, Oslo
1999	PICTURES 1986 – 1997	Drassanes, Valencia
1999	PICTURES 1991 – 1997	Ormeau Baths Gallery, Belfast
1999	THE RUDIMENTARY PICTURES	Milton Keynes Gallery, Milton Keynes
1999	NINETEEN NINETY NINE	Kunstmuseum, Bonn
2000	NINETEEN NINETY NINE	Museum Moderner Kunst, Vienna
2000	NINETEEN NINETY NINE	Museum of Contemporary Art, Chicago
2000	MM 2000, BIENNALE DE LYON	Halle Tony Garnier, Lyon
2001	GILBERT & GEORGE	Chateau d'Arenton, Alex
2001	THE ART OF GILBERT & GEORGE	The Factory, Athens School of Art, Athens
2002	THE DIRTY WORDS PICTURES	Serpentine Gallery, London
2002	NINE DARK PICTURES	Portikus, Frankfurt
2002	GILBERT & GEORGE	Centro Cultural de Belém, Lisbon
2002	GILBERT & GEORGE	Kunsthaus Bregenz, Austria
2004	TWENTY LONDON EAST ONE PICTURES	Musee d'Art Moderne, Saint-Etienne
2005	GINKGO PICTURES	Venice Biennale, Venice
2005	TWENTY LONDON EAST ONE PICTURES	Kestnergesellschaft, Hanover
2006	SONOFAGOD PICTURES: Was Jesus Heterosexual?	Bonnefanten Museum, Maastricht
2007	MAJOR EXHIBITION	Tate Modern, London
2007	MAJOR EXHIBITION	Haus der Kunst, Munich
2007	MAJOR EXHIBITION	Castello di Rivoli, Turin
2008	MAJOR EXHIBITION	Milwaukee Art Museum, Milwaukee
2008	MAJOR EXHIBITION	De Young Museum, San Francisco
2008	MAJOR EXHIBITION	Brooklyn Museum, New York
2008	NOTATIONS: GILBERT AND GEORGE	Philadelphia Museum of Art, Philadelphia
2010	JACK FREAK PICTURES	Centro de Arte Contemporãneo, Malaga
2010	JACK FREAK PICTURES	Museum of Contemporary Art, Zagreb
2010	THE PAINTINGS (WITH US IN NATURE) 1971	Kröller-Müller Museum, Otterlo
2010	JACK FREAK PICTURES	The Centre for Fine Arts, Brussels
2011	JACK FREAK PICTURES	Deichtorhallen, Hamburg
2011	JACK FREAK PICTURES	Lentos Art Museum, Linz
2011	THE URETHRA POSTCARD PICTURES	Ivorypress Art + Books, Madrid
2011	JACK FREAK PICTURES	Laznia Centre for Contemporary Art, Gdańsk
2011	THE URETHRA POSTCARD PICTURES	Pinacotela Giovanni e Marella Agnelli, Torino
2013	LONDON PICTURES	Museum Küppersmühle, Duisburg
2013	LONDON PICTURES	Casal Solleric, Palma
2014	A FAMILY COLLECTION	NMNM - Villa Paloma, Monaco
2015	GILBERT & GEORGE: THE EARLY YEARS	MOMA, New York
2015	GILBERT & GEORGE: THE ART EXHIBITION	MONA, Tasmania
2017	THE SCAPEGOATING PICTURES BERLIN	St. Matthaüs Church Berlin
2017	SCAPEGOATING PICTURES	Ludwig museum, Budapest
2018	SCAPEGOATING PICTURES	The MAC, Belfast
2018	THE GREAT EXHIBITION	LUMA, Arles
2018	GILBERT & GEORGE MAJOR EXHIBITION	HAM, Helsinki
2019	THE GREAT EXHIBITION	Moderna Museet, Stockholm
2019	THE GREAT EXHIBITION	Astrup Fearnley Museet, Oslo
2020	THE GREAT EXHIBITION	LUMA Westbau + Kunsthalle Zurich, Zurich
2020	THE LOCARNO EXHIBITION	Pinacoteca Comunale Casa Rusca
2020	THE GREAT EXHIBITION	Reykjavik Art Museum, Iceland
2021	THE GREAT EXHIBITION	Schirn Kunsthalle, Frankfurt

INDEX TO NEW NORMAL PICTURE TITLES

Published to accompany the exhibition

GILBERT & GEORGE
NEW NORMAL PICTURES

30 MAY to 31 JULY 2021

Produced by Hurtwood, London
Printed and bound in Great Britain

ISBN13: 978-2-9100-5596-7

Thaddaeus Ropac
69 Avenue du Général Leclerc
Paris
FR-93500 Pantin

ropac.net